**Dr Selina Stone** is a Post Education at Durham U host of the *Sunday School for Misfits* podcast, and a sought-after speaker and preacher. She is author of *The Spirit and the Body: Towards a womanist Pentecostal social justice ethic* (Brill and Schöningh, 2023). Her previous roles include Lecturer in Theology at St Mellitus College and Community Organiser and Programme Director at the Centre for Theology and Community. Selina is a proud Brummie, sister to Daniel, Matthew and Joanna, and daughter of Mark and Millicent (RIEP).

# TARRY AWHILE

Wisdom from Black spirituality
for people of faith

## THE ARCHBISHOP OF CANTERBURY'S LENT BOOK 2024

Selina Stone

First published in Great Britain in 2023

Society for Promoting Christian Knowledge
SPCK Group, The Record Hall, 16–16A Baldwin's Gardens, London, EC1N 7RJ
www.spck.org.uk

British Library Cataloguing-in-Publication Data
A catalogue record for this book is available from the British Library

ISBN 978–0–281–09010–5
eBook ISBN 978–0–281–09011–2

1 3 5 7 9 10 8 6 4 2

Typeset by Fakenham Prepress Solutions, Fakenham, Norfolk, NR21 8NL
First printed in Great Britain by Clays Ltd, Bungay, NR35 1ED
eBook by Fakenham Prepress Solutions, Fakenham, Norfolk, NR21 8NL

Produced on paper from sustainable sources

For all of us who struggle as we tarry

# Contents

# Contents

# Foreword

There is a hauntingly beautiful Taizé song that echoes the words of Christ in Gethsemane: 'Stay with me. Remain here with me; watch and pray.' In the Taizé tradition, I have repeated the words of this chant over and over, until I feel I can almost hear the plea of Christ through the notes, as though I am brought face to face with his suffering.

In many ways, Christ's words in Gethsemane are the call we follow throughout the days of Lent: 'My soul is overwhelmed with sorrow to the point of death. Stay here and keep watch with me' (Matthew 26:38). We are tasked with waiting on Christ in the painful hours of the night, in the liminal space where the joy of the resurrection is still far off, in the difficult times of death and devastation.

In this wonderful, insightful book, Dr Selina Stone draws on the tradition of 'tarrying': staying with the Lord, bringing the wisdom of Black spirituality to bear on our individual and collective waitings on Christ. What tarrying does, as Selina makes clear, is open the possibility for genuine encounter, with God and between ourselves.

The sense of presence she recounts includes not just individual, but also collective presence; not just awareness found alone in quiet contemplation, but also awareness of the injustice and suffering that cries out in our world. Tarrying gives us an opportunity to rest; to be restored in the arms of God and by the support of our communities. It gives us the opportunity to see the realities of the world more clearly, and to imagine more boldly what the world could be.

There is a sense of waiting, perhaps waiting longer than expected or hoped for, which speaks not just to the Lenten experience, but very much to the Black experience over centuries of persecution and oppression. As we wait on the Lord, we often feel as if we are still living with the burdens and suffering from which his death has liberated us. For many of us, the Lenten season lasts beyond Lent. We continue to cry out 'How long, O Lord?' Tarrying calls us not to look away, to close our eyes or to ignore, but to remain present in the pain as Christ implores us. And yet there remains the hope, the expectation, that the promised day of justice is coming, that all will be redeemed and made new; a promise that fills us with inner strength and binds us to one another, even when the world imputes weakness and tries to tear us apart.

The season of Lent, besides one of waiting, can also be considered a journey of healing, as Dr Stone contemplates. It can be a time to rise together from the cold dust of Ash Wednesday into the eternal life of Easter Sunday. It can be an opportunity to see our lives, incomplete and unpredictable, reflected and made meaningful by the characters of Scripture and the story of God's people. Dr Stone offers new biblical reflections grounded in ancient wisdom, recognising the hopes and fears of those who tarry on the Lord in the long season of waiting.

I pray that you find this book a hopeful, compassionate place to rest awhile during Lent. However you are waiting, whatever you are waiting with, I pray you would be filled with the certainty of God's presence. May you be accompanied, as you wait, by brothers and sisters in Christ who encourage and support you. May you meet and be transformed by the Lord of lords, whose day is truly near.

+ + *Justin Cantuar*
Lambeth Palace, London

# Acknowledgements

First I give honour to God, who is the source of all life, and whose grace made not only this book possible, but also all of the learning and wisdom within it.

I would like to extend my thanks to my dear friends Carlton, Akeem, Shavaun and Father Simon, who read drafts, listened to long voice notes and helped me sharpen my ideas. I cannot thank you enough for giving your time during the three months in which I attempted to put such huge ideas and experiences into writing. Huge thanks to Alison Barr at SPCK for providing comments and feedback which helped me to clarify and simplify the many ideas I threw at you at various points! And thanks to project editor Joy Tibbs, copy-editor Nicki Copeland and proofreader Rima Devereaux for their close reading of the manuscript, and their helpful comments and suggestions. I would also like to thank Professor Mike Higton at Durham who recognised that it would be a good idea for me to write this book, gave me space to complete it and also read it through for me.

My ultimate thanks go to my parents who took responsibility for teaching me the faith in word and deed, and to their parents who did the same for them. Special thanks to the Black Pentecostal church I grew up in, which was my second family and provided me with lifelong friends. For every pastor, elder, youth leader, intercessor, catering team member and Sunday school teacher who helped to build this community – I am because of you. For everyone who prayed and continues to pray for me as I journey – I owe you more than I can put into words.

# Introduction

Tarry ye here, and watch with me.
(Matthew 26:38, KJV)

Thousands of years ago, in the motherland of Africa, humanity was born. On this, scientists are in agreement, and the biblical creation narratives do not deny this possibility. It is not clear where the Garden of Eden is precisely, but rivers are described as flowing from this garden into modern-day East Africa and the Middle East.[1] Africa is home for all of us. In the centuries that have followed, human beings have evolved into various shades and shapes, with different facial features, cultures and languages. Some left the womb of humanity to migrate around the globe at will, to establish different societies. Others would remain in the place where it all began, and kingdoms and queendoms would emerge. In all places, we sought to understand the world in which we lived, developed new technologies, and explored our connection with God and with one another. We have formed so many expressions of what it is to be human. Nevertheless, in Africa, we share a common human origin, and also a deep, spiritual link. The spiritual wisdom and faith of those we would now describe as African, or African descendants, will be the theme of this book.

I write this book as an African Caribbean woman born and raised in Birmingham. I am the granddaughter of four formidable Jamaicans who arrived in Birmingham in 1963. They raised their children in the working-class inner city where my parents were born, got married and raised me and my siblings. I grew up as a Pentecostal Christian, which means this tradition is core to my experience of Christianity and of Black people's faith. But my understanding of both would expand and grow in subsequent years. My introduction to the Church of England came primarily through my church primary school, but most significantly through community organising in an Anglo-Catholic parish in Brixton. My understanding of the kinds of Christianity Black people identify with was broadened in this place as I watched a Black woman, in robes, lead this majority-Black congregation. The breadth of what we think of as Black spirituality will, I hope, be expanded in the course of this book.

But why do we need to talk specifically about 'Black' spirituality or faith? These are ways of naming the beliefs, practices and emphases that emerge when, as Black people, we think, talk about and live out our faith in Jesus in ways that are authentic to us. This book is an exploration of some of these elements. I capitalise 'Black' to be clear that I am talking about people of African descent who often share certain social, cultural and/or political experiences. Black people in the UK identify mainly as African, African Caribbean or mixed Black heritage. But globally there are significant Black populations in Latin America and North America, and many Black people who live in the Middle East, Asia and elsewhere.

Black people's experiences vary according to class, gender, sexuality, disability, generation, migration and geography, among other factors. Black people, like white people, may share ancestral roots but do not automatically share the same views, ideas or experiences of life or Christianity. It would be impossible to cover the whole range of Black spiritual perspectives in this book or to summarise them simply. My hope is simply to introduce some of the wisdom that is available when we learn from the ways Black people encounter and have encountered God.

There are many contexts in which, as Black people, we are prevented from living out an authentic faith that is relevant to us culturally, socially and even politically. In some contexts this can be subtle, and in others more explicit. It might involve suppressing preferred forms of worship, rituals or expression in order to conform to the expectations of white Christian spirituality and faith. It can affect us when we are asked to quieten the urgent questions and concerns that shape our lived experiences as Black people in the world, in order to be considered part of the community. This is, of course, damaging to Black people when we remain in such spaces. But it also robs the Church of the wisdom that God might provide through Black people's stories, theologies, testimonies and faith. Black people have always, in the UK and elsewhere, found spaces in which to preserve the spiritual perspectives and practices that enable us to meet God amid our particular experiences. In such contexts, our hearts are healed, our souls are enriched and our bodies find a space to belong.

It is common for us to think of Black people's circumstances as shaped primarily by oppression, but this does a disservice to Black people and to God who is present with us. This is not a book about suffering, struggle or racism, or even racial justice, though these issues will come up at various points. Black faith and spirituality should not be considered primarily as a response or a strategy to address such issues, even if, historically and in the present, faith has helped Black people to endure. Black faith and spirituality are what they are because of the kindness of God who meets us, upholds us and sustains us through joys, storms, laughter and trials, individually and collectively. This encounter is the core interest of this book. It is an encounter that overturns the sin of racism, opposes racial suffering and trauma, and leads us towards a just future. However, it is much more than this. It is an encounter that surprises us in unexpected places, reorients how we view reality and ourselves as a whole and leads us through our many movements as individuals and as communities. It is an encounter with the Spirit who empowers the unlikely person; stimulates singing, shouting and quiet; brings healing and turns weeping into joy.

# Introduction

Tarrying is a particular spiritual practice within many Black churches, especially Pentecostal congregations. It is a collective time of waiting on God which can go on for hours, and involves people from across all groupings of age, class, gender, ethnicity, physicality or status. It recognises the interdependence of the individual and the community for encounter with God. It is a time of surrender to God, in the hope of personal and communal transformation. It is also a moment for intercession, for bringing our personal needs to God as well as our loving concern for our neighbours and the world. Tarrying is important for all of us who live with desire, loss, weakness, temptation, frustration, disappointment and fear. It provides us with space to face our creatureliness, our struggles, our humanity and our mortality. It allows us to confess, to tell the truth and to lay bare the matters we push under the rug to deal with 'another time', which often never arrives. It allows us time to ponder the ways of God that are not our ways and our lives within the life of God. It can be uncomfortable, as it brings to the surface things we would rather not see.

But if we are open as we tarry, the Spirit of God may come to examine our hearts and lives and invite us to let go or take up, to tear down or build. As we face the weight of our human experience and our lives in all their complexity, we might be overwhelmed. But in this, we do not need to fear. For as we sit in the presence of God who looks upon us with delight, we find ourselves tarrying with and for one who is familiar with our weaknesses. We do not sit with a wrathful enemy, but a righteous judge who seeks to draw us ever closer to Godself. It is through the Spirit of God that we might be drawn to confession, to repentance, to repairing what is in our power to address, and to walk in newness of life with Christ and one another.

By entering into the particularity of Black faith and spirituality in this book, we will stumble across what is common to us all as human beings. If you are not a Black person reading this book, you may well recognise aspects of what I describe from your own experiences of life, faith and spirituality. This is because whatever we share honestly as human beings from our particular context will often resonate with those who on the surface may seem different from us. There are many overlapping types of experiences and opportunities for solidarity as we listen to one another across our human family. For some of you reading, this will be the first time you have read a book on faith and spirituality that feels like home. You will not have to jump through many hoops, trying to interpret unfamiliar language or concepts or look up cultural references that are not your own. Welcome, breathe and enjoy. For others, this may be the first time, or perhaps one of a few times, when you will have to do some reflective work to join the dots with your own experience. The stories, ideas, reflections and even some of the language may not be familiar, and you may find it challenging to find your place. I invite you not to be put off by this: great treasures await us as we remain curious and open to finding God in the unfamiliar.

# 1

# Darkness

Now the earth was formless and empty, darkness was over the surface of the deep, and the Spirit of God was hovering over the waters.

And God said, 'Let there be light,' and there was light. (Genesis 1:2–3)

I have always found the creation narratives of Genesis fascinating because of how they stimulate the imagination. The story begins with darkness. We are usually encouraged to see darkness negatively. Even in this passage, darkness goes with formlessness and emptiness. Darkness is linked to what is not yet what it could be or should be. Darkness is often something we are desperate to change. In our day-to-day lives, we know that darkness can be dangerous, for a range of reasons. In a purely practical sense, we can be more easily hurt in the dark. In public, a road without streetlights puts drivers and pedestrians at risk. Moving around your house at night in the dark will almost always result in a stubbed toe. It is easier to steal, attack or vandalise in the dark. Darkness covers many kinds of evil deeds.

We also use the word 'darkness' to discuss what we consider to be difficult in our day-to-day speech. We speak about 'dark times' in our lives or the world at large. We might talk about 'dark thoughts' as the kinds of ideas that lead us to anxiety, despair or depression, or even to harm ourselves or others. Darkness is not something we want; it is something we endure.

Moreover, darkness is used as a metaphor for confusion, separation from God and sinfulness in various parts of the

Scriptures. Talking about Christ or Christians as the 'light of the world' presumes that the world is dark, and that this darkness is bad. Those 'living in darkness' (Matthew 4:16) are those who are somehow outside God's light, which they must encounter. Those who love darkness, in the Gospel of John, are said to do so because 'their deeds [are] evil' (John 3:19).

The light versus dark binary can be helpful to some extent in helping to illustrate spiritual or theological ideas. But trying to force everything into such a binary can be unhelpful. Life can be surprisingly grey, as can people and our actions. More often than not, even the actions, words or behaviours we see or emulate are a combination of things: not entirely pure or wholly corrupt, but somewhere in the middle. We may have a 'light' intention that can have a 'dark' effect despite our best efforts.

But we have to be mindful of how use of language can affect how we view and treat one another. It is so easy to begin to categorise people as 'good' (light) and 'evil' (dark). We can easily reduce people to being one or the other, with the former being worthy of our trust and the latter deserving of our suspicion. Our brains are wired to simplify processes by making these kinds of shortcuts. This is what we often call 'unconscious bias'. But they cause us to fail in our relationship with others and even with ourselves. It can be an even bigger challenge to remember that we cannot categorise ourselves as 'good' or 'evil'. We cannot be summed up by referring either to the best thing we have ever done or to the worst thing.

This general tendency to categorise people can also influence our social dynamics. Race, which categorises humanity in a hierarchy of 'light' at the top and 'dark' at the bottom, could be seen as a prime example of the problems of this binary thinking. Although we may know in theory that spiritual darkness in the Scriptures is not about the spirituality of darker-skinned people, we can find it very difficult to separate the two. I say 'we' because this is something that affects all of us. As Black people formed by European thought, we are also at risk of seeing ourselves as 'dark', empty and formless. Instinctively, we might be tempted to judge the spiritual practices of African people more harshly than the spirituality of white Europeans. We might imagine African forms of Christianity to be less godly, reasonable or sophisticated (if sophistication is an objective we think matters). I have even heard it said (erroneously) that Black people do not have or care for 'real theology' or 'proper' interpretation of the Scriptures. We are trapped in a binary where light (and white) is closer to goodness and dark (or Black) is inferior.

One historic example of this is in the description of Africa as 'the dark continent'. This was a colonial way of describing Africa which communicated various ideas. First, the various African tribes and peoples were darker-skinned than the Europeans who arrived. Second, Africa was a mysterious place with many unknown elements in terms of geography, climate, culture, religions, languages and history. But it was also a condescending title that communicated the notion that Africa lacked enlightenment, knowledge, progress and excellence. It was a *theological* label, suggesting that it was a place absent of God's presence and light. A light that would be brought by white Europeans. This belief in the 'darkness' of Africa has historically legitimised all manner of violence and savagery by Europeans. The Pope's blessing of Christians to enslave, kill, pillage and oppress indigenous peoples across Latin America, Africa, Asia, Oceania and beyond was owing to this belief in the spiritual darkness of such places (as well as greed for their resources and land).[1]

But this idea of 'dark' and 'light' places does not only occur in history. Today, in our contemporary world, there are places and people we are encouraged to see as spiritually dark, as those further from God than others. In our conversations about inner cities and estates we can find traces of this. Those who have been or are serving time in prison, or those people involved or at risk of involvement in serious crimes, also exist in this category. We might imagine spiritual darkness characterising the streets where youth violence has become so prevalent, or in the areas where poverty has ravaged communities. But these are also spaces where communities come together to care for those who are lonely and to welcome the refugee and the migrant. These are spaces where communities come together for festivals, to protest against police murders and to donate provisions to those who face food poverty. To presume that God is absent, that God's light is not present in such spaces, is a grave error.

But in our contemporary contexts, we also find reminders of this fear of the dark in culture, whether Christian or not. In so many of the works of Western art that are gazed at daily in museums or in stained-glass windows in churches each week, these binaries persist. As Chine McDonald has explained in dialogue with historian David Olusoga:

> At certain points in history, it may have been just as shocking to say that God is not a white man as it would have been to suggest that the devil is not Black ... During [the Elizabethan period] the darkness of the devil's skin was described as Black as an African's – just like mine. The colour white however, 'by contrast was the marker of purity, virginity and even divinity'.[2]

Jesus and the disciples, though Middle Eastern, are almost always depicted as pale-skinned and European. The angels too. But darkness is devilish. This pattern in art can be traced socially, in how cultures around the world respond to those of darker complexions. 'Colourism' means that darker-skinned people, even within Black, Asian, Latin American or indigenous communities, experience prejudice and exclusion. On an island such as Jamaica, where my grandparents are from, it is well known that, historically, those of lighter complexion have often had access to more secure, better paid and more senior employment. Skin tone becomes a marker of class in many contexts. Skin-lightening creams sell across the world, owing to the racist lie that 'lighter is better'. Hurt can occur within families as people make careless comments or treat lighter-skinned members of the family better than those with a darker skin tone. People can even choose (and not choose) partners with some concern for the skin tone their children might have. Such is the depth of the harm that permeates so many aspects of our lives together.

But we do not have to take such an approach to understanding darkness and light. We can resist the assumption that darkness should be understood as emptiness or evil and connected to Black life in particular. Darkness and God are not incompatible. God exists in the beginning in the darkness. Darkness is not a threat to God, nor is God afraid of it. The Spirit is content to hover in the dark over the surface of the deep. And then God, who is later revealed to comprise multiple persons ('Let *us* make human beings', Genesis 1:26 NLT), begins to speak. God who is Spirit utters her words and the material world fulfils what God's words have been sent to accomplish. God says, 'Let there be light' (Genesis 1:3), and light appears out of nowhere. God sees that the light is good – it is as it should be – and God gives it a name (Genesis 1:4–5). God's desire to create is simply for the sake of delight. God, the source of life and all that exists, hangs out in the darkness and then, like an artist looking at an untouched canvas, thinks, 'What might we create here?' God is not afraid of the darkness, nor does God resent it. There is no record of God condemning the darkness or cursing it; God simply imagines what good can come from it, and brings it forth.

Darkness is, after all, essential to life. Those of us who ever grew cress at school will remember that it is in the darkness that particular forms of plant life grow. Light can disrupt the rhythms of plant life. It is in the darkness that we rest, our bodies recharge and our brains restore themselves. Light, when we are tired, keeps us awake and keeps us from the sleep we need to be healthy. Light can be stark and unwelcome when we need gentleness and softness. Darkness is crucial to the development of particular species, which need space to hide away and hibernate. It is especially important for the young of various mammals (including humans) who grow in the darkness of the womb. Coming into the light too quickly can mean long-term health issues or even premature death.

In the Scriptures, light can also deceive, with Satan being described as one who appears as 'an angel of light' (2 Corinthians 11:14). We are warned, therefore, that we cannot always trust the 'light'.

Darkness, on the other hand, is the exciting starting point of creation, as we have seen. It is like a stage curtain, keeping things hidden until the appropriate time. Darkness represents a place and time that is full of potential, expectation and anticipation. And in the darkness of Genesis, God is.

## Questions for reflection

1 In your own language and perspectives, do you resonate with how we can develop a suspicion or fear of darkness?

2 Can you see connections between the fear and suspicion of darkness and attitudes you or others have regarding people of African descent, or of other people who are not considered to be 'light', either physically or in terms of their culture and ways of being?

3 What difference might it make to form more positive ideas about darkness or 'dark' places for mission and ministry?

# Black and Christian

On a long and dusty road, the chariot moved along, pulled by two horses who were at risk of being exhausted by the heat. The road between Jerusalem and Gaza was bumpy and treacherous, but inside this chariot, this passenger had other things on his mind. He had just been among those who worship Yahweh the God of Israel, at the festival. His heart was full, being with those from many corners of the earth who were descendants of Abraham and Sarah, Isaac and Rebekah, and Jacob and Leah, Rachel, Bilhah and Zilpah. He himself had been permitted to leave the royal court of his Queen, who ruled over the southern region of the Nile, to attend the festival. And he longed to return to share with his own people what he had experienced.

They stopped for a break on the way, for the horses to be watered and his driver to have a nap. As he waited in his chariot, he began to read the scroll containing the words of the prophet Isaiah. Out of the corner of his eye, he saw a man appear by the chariot. He paused for a moment, wondering if he knew the man who was staring at him. No, he didn't. How long had he been standing there? Was it a trap set up by bandits? Did this man need help?

The man caught his breath and then said, 'Hi, I am Philip, a disciple of Jesus. I heard you reading the prophet's words – do you know what they mean?'

The Ethiopian eunuch, as he is called by Luke (Acts 8:27), represents an important starting point as we reflect on faith and spirituality within Black people's lives. In some ways, he is a predictable candidate for bringing the gospel to Africa. He is a man with a significant position in a royal court, an important figure in his nation's government. He has some wealth, since he is travelling in a chariot and can afford such things as a scroll with the prophet's words written on them. He is part of the elite in his country. Yet in another way, he is unpredictable: he is potentially a Gentile and definitely a eunuch. Scholars cannot agree on whether or not he is an African Jew. He is coming back from a Jewish festival and is reading the Jewish Scriptures, but it is not stated that he is Jewish. Either way, he is noticeably different, an outsider, as Zorodzai Dube explains:

> The eunuch of our story travelled from Ethiopia to Jerusalem, which prompts our imagination of a foreigner in a foreign land. How was he received? How did he himself react to the challenges that faced him in this foreign culture? In the ancient world, the term Ethiopia signified a region beyond the borders, a place having mostly negative connotations ... We can imagine that his dark skin may have rendered the Ethiopian court official a conspicuous person. If he wanted to hide his identity and mingle anonymously with the inhabitants and pilgrims in Jerusalem, he would soon be recognised as a foreigner due to the colour of his skin – the indelible ink that marked him as an outsider.[1]

The Ethiopian eunuch is not the kind of person who can blend in or is assumed to belong. He is visibly different because he is African in a Middle Eastern context, but also because of his gender. Luke describes him time and time again in the story as 'the eunuch', putting this aspect of his identity front and centre (Acts 8:26–39). Luke doesn't get into the details of what this status means, but he thinks it is important for us to know. Many royal courts would employ men to work for them and would castrate them to prevent any risk of royal lines being 'contaminated' through sexual activity between them and any of the women they worked for. The men in power would have sex with whomever they wanted, of course, including with eunuchs. But other men posed a risk that needed to be addressed. Eunuchs were often considered effeminate, not really men, or somewhere in between women and men because of their physical condition.[2] Eunuchs did not fit into the usual boxes.

As a eunuch, this Ethiopian may have faced some challenges in being accepted by the Jewish community. In Leviticus 21:20 the law states that men with 'damaged testicles' cannot be priests. In Deuteronomy 23:1 we read, 'No one who has been emasculated by crushing or cutting may enter the assembly of the LORD.' This could mean that, although he went to worship, if anyone had identified him as a eunuch, he might not have been allowed to take part. In some cases, he may have been permitted to worship in a section of the temple reserved for women, foreigners and others who were considered unclean.

But despite this, there was also some hope for eunuchs in the Jewish tradition. In the book of Isaiah (which Luke tells us the traveller is conveniently reading at the time), we find a promise from God for eunuchs:

I will give within my temple and its walls
 a memorial and a name
 better than sons and daughters;
I will give them an everlasting name
 that will endure for ever.
(Isaiah 56:5)

I wonder whether he found this scripture on purpose on his way back from Jerusalem. Was he turned away because of his visible difference? Did he go back to the Scriptures to remind himself of how God viewed him, despite how he had been treated by the people of God? Either way, this passage reminds him, and us, that God's thoughts are not our thoughts. Where religious tradition meant that this person was unclean and should be kept away from the community, this promise brought him right to the centre of God's loving embrace. In the temple, the place of ultimate holiness and worship, God will write the names of eunuchs. God promises them a status that those able to have children will not be able to rival. The role of the Ethiopian eunuch in beginning the story of Christianity among African people may well be representative of this promise being fulfilled. He has gone down in history.

The Ethiopian eunuch represents Black Christianity, not only because he is African, but also because his story represents the faith that emerges among people and within places considered godless and empty. Black Christianity is a faith that begins in the spaces that are unknown or rejected by the mainstream, in the overlooked places. The Ethiopian eunuch is recognised as the first to bring Christianity to Africa in around AD 37. John Mark, the author of the second Gospel, is understood to have established the first African church we know about in around AD 42.

It is to these figures that thanks are due for the initial sharing of the message of Jesus in these parts. In them, the message of the gospel arrived without violence or force, even if future empires would utilise such means in their eagerness to convert through dominance. In Africa, Christianity is understood to have taken root in Egypt, Alexandria to be specific, before a second wave spread in Ethiopia. The story goes that Christianity was brought into the Ethiopian royal courts by two young men who were asked to support the king of Axum, Ezana, on behalf of his mother. Ezana would become Africa's first Christian king.[3] Gayraud Wilmore goes on to explain:

By 580, Christianity had become the official religion of the three Nubian [Southern Egyptian] Kingdoms, and a Byzantine [eastern Roman as opposed to western Roman] form of the faith triumphantly raised the cross over the holy places and shrines of the former African Traditional Religion in the heartland of Black Africa ... That story is an essential element of what we might call the 'first visit' of Christianity to Africa – extending across a period of six hundred years from the conversation of the Ethiopian eunuch in about AD 37 and the coming of John Mark to Alexandria a few years later to the courageous mission of Longinus to the people of Alwa in Upper Nubia during the second half of the sixth century ... Christianity took root in the Upper Nile Valley, and the Black churches and monasteries of Nubia flourished for more than eight hundred years.[4]

This is an often entirely unknown aspect of Christian history, particularly for those of us who have only been taught about the arrival of Christianity through European missionaries and colonialism. It was fifteen centuries later that the Portuguese would arrive on the shores of the 'new world'. Blessed by the Pope, they sought to Christianise the 'heathens' they would encounter on their explorations. In the course of the following century and beyond, the Spanish, English, Dutch, French, Belgians and Germans would follow suit. Driven not by a genuine love for the peoples of the world, but rather by a lust for power and wealth, they brought the sword and the Bible with them across the globe. These encounters with European Christianity were secondary, and unnecessary in light of the Ethiopian eunuch's story.

Similarly, in the case of India, it was centuries after St Thomas is understood to have brought Christianity to that country that Europeans sought to enforce another version. Europeans arrived in 'dark' parts of the world, assuming that God was not there and that even if God had been there, global peoples needed Europeans to help them find God.

If we are honest, Luke's account of the story of the Ethiopian eunuch could also serve to further such an idea. Zorodzai Dube queries Philip's attitude, suggesting it is condescending:

Using the reference to the Spirit to legitimate and buffer his boldness, Philip proceeds as the (only) one who is enlightened. He has the right understanding of the Scriptures, and he has the authority to decide whether there are any hindrances for the Ethiopian's baptism ... this is, in my view, a story about the outsider who wants to be regarded as insider. In the same way, today's immigrants yearn to be included into the cultures and identities of their host countries. We may wonder why the eunuch – seemingly so uncritically – accepted the epistemological premise of Philip's interpretation. Why did he not debate Philip's understanding of the text? I think that in this situation the eunuch acted like most immigrants who continuously yearn for acceptance and who are willing to barter their cultural heritage for the sake of peace and social acceptance.[5]

This can feel like a difficult perspective on this story. After all, haven't I been saying that this is an important element of the history of the Church? If that is the case, how can I also entertain such a critical perspective? Well, multiple things can be true. It is true that this story can go a good way to showing Africans as early recipients of the gospel, and early evangelists. It can disprove histories that suggest Christianity would never have arrived in Africa without the help of ships and guns from Europe. But it can also, because of how Luke tells the story, be used to reinforce the idea that Africans cannot come to the truth about God without help. It might also, drawing on some of the pre-existing ideas we have about 'dark Africa', suggest that Africans in particular cannot discern the truth unless someone from a different racial group tells them what to think. This might not be the first thought we have, and this was not at all what Luke wanted to communicate. Nevertheless, these kinds of ideas can lurk in our subconscious and affect our lived relationships and practice.

Historically, European Christians have acted out of such assumptions, imagining that Africans could not be Christian without first trying their utmost to become as similar to white

Europeans as possible. Despite the many spiritual traditions, perspectives and practices Africans developed, including African churches and forms of Christianity, Europeans always considered Africans to be spiritual students rather than teachers. The colonial catastrophe that resulted from these ways of being was destructive of African people's spiritualities, cultures, social relationships, political orders and psychological and mental well-being. The effects continue to reverberate for communities in the African diaspora today who remain disconnected from our heritage and history. African cultures cannot be assumed to be anti-Christian, nor are African peoples further away from God than white people. These ideas can continue to influence us today, in terms of who we view as teachers, preachers and spiritual leaders, even within churches that have many people from different backgrounds.

## Questions for reflection

1 What are your own reflections on the story of the Ethiopian eunuch, and how does this narrative affect your ideas about the beginnings of the Christian faith among African people?
2 How does this story shape your understanding of the Church, especially in terms of the inclusion of those who are visibly different and do not fit into the categories many of us are used to?

# Tarrying in the dark

For Black Christianity that emerges from within overlooked places, certain spiritual practices have importance. I am talking here very particularly about the kinds of Christian traditions that develop when Black people come together and can be themselves. One of these practices is 'tarrying'. Tarrying, as I said in the introduction, is a spiritual practice found within the context of Black churches of different traditions. It is simply a time to wait on God. It is rooted in the Gospel narratives where, on the night of Jesus' arrest, he asks his sleepy disciples, 'Could you not tarry with me, even for an hour?' (Matthew 26:40, my paraphrase). This spiritual practice seeks to offer an undeniable 'yes'. Through this practice, the faithful are able to write a new story. Rather than leaving Jesus lonely in his time of longing for spiritual companionship, he is met in the tarrying moment by a whole host of friends, ready to accompany him.

In reality, tarrying can continue for much longer than an hour, despite Jesus only asking for that in the Gospels. At the church I attended when I was growing up, we would have half-night prayer meetings and all-night prayer meetings, beginning at 6 p.m. and ending at midnight or 6 a.m. the next day. These services would involve singing both learned songs and spontaneous songs inspired by the presence of the Holy Spirit. People would read scriptural passages that stuck in their minds as important for the community. Spontaneous sermons and words of encouragement were all expected and shared in this space. Prayers for healing, intercessions and anointing with oil would also frequently take place. People would also tarry for the gift of speaking in tongues. David Daniels III describes it this way:

In tarrying God [is] acknowledged as sovereign, deciding who to save as well as when and where … God decides who

19

should receive callings as ministers, missionaries, teachers, and prayer leaders. God sends dreams, visions, prophecies, an inner witness, and other forms of guidance to communicate God's will to congregations and individuals. In tarrying people are instructed to let God have God's way in them. They are taught how to yield to the Holy Spirit, how to let God take charge. They are encouraged to transfer this disposition to other areas of their Christian life ... tarrying expressed the yoking of divine and human agency with the primacy of divine initiative being recognised.[1]

Tarrying is an open spiritual practice, whereby those people often considered to be less important in our spiritual communities and the world at large are brought to the centre. A tarrying service is a space often led by women. Women make up the majority of church communities across the board, and these spaces are places where they exercise their ministry as spiritual leaders of the community. It is the grandmothers and the aunties that you hope will intercede for you in this space. The spiritual power of women is not denied. They speak with authority, they pray with great faith and they are bold in their testimony.

Tarrying is a space where young people and children are included and prayed for. Those present are prayed for fervently, for God's protection and guidance in their lives. They might even be asked to pray aloud for the whole church, and are encouraged to share words for the congregation. Those who are absent are not missed out; their names and needs are held up in prayer to God. This is especially the case when particular incidents happen that affect young people.

Tarrying is a space in which the fathers and mothers of the community are given honour and the opportunity to share their wisdom. It is an intergenerational affair. In this space, the wrinkled hands of a grandmother or a grandfather might reach out to you, to hold your hand and pray for your future. The microphone will be carried to one who has prayed countless prayers, so that they may utter one more in your hearing.

Tarrying is a time to wait *with* God and to wait *on* God. To wait *with* God is to recognise that, in the tarrying service, we are setting time aside to meet with the one who is the source of our life. It is to pause and sit with the one who has made us and who sustains us. It is to sit shoulder to shoulder with Jesus, to be looked upon by God and to be filled ever more with the Holy Spirit.

To wait *on* God is to continually notice our need for God to hear, to speak and to act. It is a response to lament; we wait on God because we wait for God to answer. In this posture, we expect that this time will not be in vain, but we will leave having received something from the one who has all things to give. It may simply be a word of encouragement, insight or hope. It could be an instruction, a new conviction, a new vocation. It might be a spiritual gift, or even a miraculous intervention that reminds you, like Hagar, that God is the one who sees (see Genesis 16:13). Tarrying is a gathered practice that enlivens the individual. We cannot tarry alone.

Tarrying is, therefore, an important practice to frame our whole lives, regardless of our ethnic identity or cultural background. We all find ourselves, whether or not we want to, in a place of waiting. In all kinds of ways, we feel the loss of what we hope for. This can range from the desires we have for our personal lives to the big ideas we have about the way the world should be. We are often waiting, and sometimes working as we wait, for a better and more just future for all.

Tarrying is something we have to choose as a practice, rather than something that is forced upon us. We might be forced to wait, but we have to choose to tarry. Tarrying represents a posture of the heart, as we have seen above. It depends on our hearts being turned towards God, while we are in a time of waiting. It includes a longing, a desperation for God's presence, God's voice, a word or an intervention. It is born from the recognition that, disconnected from the vine, we can do nothing (John 15:5).

When we return to the passage to which the practice of tarrying is linked, we find Jesus in the darkness. It is the evening when they have their meal, and afterwards:

> Jesus went with his disciples to a place called Gethsemane, and he said to them, 'Sit here while I go over there and pray.' He took Peter and the two sons of Zebedee along with him, and he began to be sorrowful and troubled. Then he said to them, 'My soul is overwhelmed with sorrow to the point of death. Stay here and keep watch with me.'
>
> Going a little farther, he fell with his face to the ground and prayed, 'My Father, if it is possible, may this cup be taken from me. Yet not as I will, but as you will.'
>
> Then he returned to his disciples and found them sleeping. 'Couldn't you men keep watch with me for one hour?' he asked Peter. 'Watch and pray so that you will not fall into temptation. The spirit is willing, but the flesh is weak.'
> (Matthew 26:36–41)

We will reflect on this from a different perspective in the final chapter, but I mention this now, to bring our attention to this particular darkness. Here Jesus is waiting on God, while he also invites his friends to wait with him and for him. This darkness is complex. It is darkness that, on the surface, appears like all the other forms of darkness we are used to. Jesus is distressed, overwhelmed with sorrow, full of anxiety. He is desperate, asking God if there is any other option. The darkness may well be disguising Jesus' own expressions of pain. The disciples seem unaware. Are they really so at ease that they could fall asleep? Do they not see the severity of the circumstances in which Jesus and they have found themselves? They seem unaware, their minds and comprehension shrouded.

In this way, this darkness is consistent with confusion, difficulty and an inability to see. Jesus seems to be caught up in what St John of the Cross calls 'the dark night of the soul'.[2] This darkness, though painful, is also full of God's sustaining grace. It is a time when we might overcome our ego and the aspects of ourselves that threaten to undermine our truest selves, as created by God. In the moment of tarrying, Jesus learns, as Daniels explains, 'how to yield to the Holy Spirit, how to let God take charge'.[3] In this darkness, Jesus gains victory over every resistance to following through with the path he has been led along. In the dark, Jesus expresses his hope, and he lays it down in the next breath.

In this sacred moment under the cover of darkness, he has time to speak to his friends for the final time. He has the space, protected from prying eyes and the evil acts of those on their way to apprehend him. He is safe in this darkness for now. And he gets to speak to his disciples, words that they need to hear: 'Watch and pray so that you will not fall into temptation. The spirit is willing, but the flesh is weak.' In the midst of darkness, Jesus calls them to watch, so that they do not fall. Spiritually, their eyes must stay open and alert because dangers are lurking. Such dangers do not appear only in the dark, but also in the light. Peter will deny Jesus three times at night when he is recognised even after sunset. When the sun rises, Jesus will be in custody and the disciples will be scattered.

Darkness is thus an opportunity for deep encounters with God, for Jesus who is longing for a way out. Tarrying in the dark is not waiting in confusion, isolation and fear. In contrast, it is a moment to turn your heart to God who specialises in working in the darkness. God receives an offering and makes a covenant with Abram in the dark (Genesis 15:12–21). It is in the dark that Jacob wrestles with God and receives a blessing (Genesis 28:10–22). It is at night that Rahab negotiates safety for her whole family

23

and earns her place in the genealogy of Jesus by hiding the spies (Joshua 2). Darkness represents deliverance for the children of Israel, separating them from the Egyptians who pursued them (Joshua 24:7). Deep darkness is one of the marks of God's presence, the place from which God's voice comes forth (Deuteronomy 4:11; 5:22–3). Darkness is the place and space of encounter with God.

By changing our minds about the darkness in so many ways, we might find a way towards anticipating that God will meet us in unexpected people, places and circumstances. This is what I hope this book will allow all of us to do: to tarry, to be open and to learn to yield to the Holy Spirit who leads us, always, to the truth.

## Questions for reflection

1 How do your own experiences of communal spiritual practice relate to tarrying within Black church tradition?
2 Are there similar intergenerational, reflective or charismatic practices that are familiar to you?
3 What significance can be found in thinking of Jesus as one who also tarried, and in the dark?

# 2

# One

As a young person growing up, I was distinctly aware of inhabiting two worlds. On the one hand was my church and my family, both very Jamaican and extremely Pentecostal. Saturday evenings meant a family film with snacks, usually in the dark, which served the dual role of creating a cinematic atmosphere and keeping the light bill low. But family fun only came after we had picked out our church clothes, ironed them and polished our shoes. I was particularly fond of the white socks with frills that looked very cute with my shiny black shoes. We said our prayers and went to bed, knowing that tomorrow would be a day for the Lord, and that meant a day of church.

On Sunday mornings, I would wake up to the smell of kidney beans boiling on the stove, in preparation for the rice and peas to be cooked when we got home after the church service. The chicken would have been seasoned the night before and left in the fridge overnight, so the smell of fresh thyme and jerk seasoning would envelop you if you ever opened the fridge between 4 p.m. on a Saturday and 2 p.m. on a Sunday. I would come down the stairs to find my mum or dad, in their dressing gown, stirring a pot of oats or cornmeal porridge. They understood that simple buttered toast or cereal would not be enough to last us through the hours between breakfast and a late lunch. This was the breakfast of long-distance runners, and our bodies would need every spoonful.

After we were all dressed, Mum would make sure our faces were shining with Vaseline or cocoa butter, and our hair was perfectly styled. As the oldest of four, I gradually became more responsible for quality control with regard to my younger siblings. Daniel was a year younger than me and could pretty much take care of himself. But Matthew, the second boy, was an extrovert who struggled to focus on the serious task of getting himself organised in time. He would often be picking on Joanna, the youngest, and thus distracting her from the most essential task of choosing the hair bobbles she wanted to wear that day.

At some point, my dad would shout to the top of the stairs, 'It's time to go,' and we would all make our way down. My mum would be putting the finishing touches to her hair or clothes while my dad tapped his foot impatiently. She would eventually arrive downstairs with a chuckle. There were more than a few Sundays of tense or argumentative drives to the house of the Lord owing to that foot-tapping.

As we pulled into the road where my church was and drove over the small hill, we would see the row of cars parked along the street signalling the path to our church. The socio-economic range of our church's membership was reflected in the varying age and shininess of the cars. Some people walked along the pavement, having taken the bus or walked from nearby. Our church was in an inner-city area which had the usual markers of socio-economic deprivation, but most of our members lived in wealthier parts of the city and drove in.

As my dad parked the car and we all got out, we would immediately hear the sound of the worship team rehearsing (on days when I wasn't already there to play my own role as a backing vocalist). The vibrations from the bass guitar could be felt through the air, and the drummer would add his own rhythm, calling passers-by to draw near. It didn't take much to get us through the doors.

As the worship team completed their warm-up, we would all begin to take our seats and the pastor would take the mic: 'Good morning, church! I was glad when they said unto me: Let us go into the House of the Lord!' Without any detectable signal, the congregation would take their cue and shout, 'Amen!' The ushers, women (and a few men) of all sizes and shades, would show people to their seats. They were always dressed as immaculately as the best air stewards with their matching uniforms and neckties. They paid special attention to the elderly who needed someone to lean on, or those nursing young children who needed to be able to step out urgently. 'Marnin', Mother Williams,' 'Marnin', Brother Stone,' 'How you do, Sister Campbell?' 'Elder Johnson, you alright?' Greetings filled with love and care could be heard amid the sung worship. People did not hesitate to walk out of their row of chairs to hug someone who had just walked in or to greet an elder at random. Expressions of care, conversations and laughter were mixed in with the moments of worship, with singing praise and giving glory to God. In this space, we were all family, all children of God.

On the other hand was the wider life I experienced from Monday to Saturday where I lived and went to school. Unlike many of my peers at church, I grew up in what many people called 'the ghetto'. It was an inner-city area, a little rough (more than a little, sometimes), but it was all I knew, and I loved it. Handsworth was such a fun place to grow up. Alongside the many African Caribbeans in Handsworth who had come to the UK in the Windrush era were people from various African countries, white British families, a huge Indian population, as well as those from Pakistan and other countries. At different times of the year, my neighbourhood was the place to be for Caribbean carnivals, Diwali festivals, Eid celebrations and Easter walks. The street where I lived would be filled with the sound of fireworks for Diwali and Eid, and Christian tracts would be pushed through letterboxes at Easter and Christmas.

My primary and secondary schools welcomed children from many of Britain's former colonies, and white Brits too. Talent shows would involve groups of girls performing songs by the Spice Girls

(I was Posh Spice in 'Who Do You Think You Are?'), Indian boys who could play the *dhol* (drum), and children with black braids, topknots and blonde curly hair taking part in drama performances.

But alongside the richness of these various communities, which lived alongside each other in general peace, many struggled to make their way through life. Parents faced the problem of finding places at good schools where their children might thrive, opportunities for secure and well-paid jobs were scarce, and poverty was constantly snapping at the heels for some. I was aware, as many were, that as children in this particular place, education, hard work and the grace of God would be our only path to a more secure future.

The world of our church communities can be vastly different from what we experience in our day-to-day lives. This can be a positive thing in some ways. Black churches have always provided a special kind of refuge in places such as the UK. Robert Beckford rightfully describes Britain's Black churches as places concerned with saving the 'lost', radical transformation, being driven by the Spirit *and* being a family.[1]

The family element has always been especially important in the earliest months and years for those arriving in Britain from the Caribbean and Africa. From Monday to Saturday, a person might be made to feel as though they did not belong. They may have had to face hostility in their workplace, in the supermarket or on the street where they lived. But on Sunday they would know they were home. Even today, in such spaces, there is no need, as a Black person, to explain your cultural nuances or worry about what others might think about your self-expression. Your face will not be misread in this place, your tone will not be misunderstood. You are free to smile, or not, to cry, shout, laugh and talk as loud as you like without fear of reprisal. Here you can let your hair down. You may struggle for dignity and recognition from nine to five, Monday to Friday, but on Sunday, you are 'a royal priesthood' (1 Peter 2:9), God's chosen, with heaven on your side.

It is no wonder people never seemed to want to leave. Church could take up the entire day, and it was meant to be so – what else should you be doing on the Lord's Day? When I was growing up, we had prayer at 9.30 a.m. (this was the spiritual warm-up), then the service from 10.30 a.m. to 1 p.m. Many Sundays we would go home to eat and nap, and then return for the evening service from 6 p.m. to 8 p.m. It was a long day.

But the gap between our church life and our wider experience can also present a challenge, when we need a faith that helps us to navigate the struggles we face. Black churches have often found ways to do this practically, by being spaces to educate children and young people, organising credit unions or supporting people to find jobs or housing. But it is also true that churches overall – and this is not unique to Black churches – can often be unaffected by the urgent issues facing not only the individuals who attend each week but also our human family as a whole. We speak about God's power, sovereignty and love, even while we witness destruction, evil and injustice all around us. We read the Scriptures, listen to sermons, are baptised and receive Holy Communion; we might even be committed to a community of Christian believers who, on the good days, become like a family to us. And yet we are also in a context where people struggle for the basic things required to live, young people are scared for their lives as they go to school, and people fleeing war have nowhere to lay their heads.

But these matters can feel as though they belong to a totally different world from that of our churches, their concerns and agendas. Entering the doors of a church can feel like walking through the back of the wardrobe into the land of Narnia. Here we find magical stories, adventurous tales and even supernatural experiences that might affect us in profound ways. And the complex and urgent issues facing us in our everyday lives can be left at the door. Returning to them after the service is over can be something like landing with a hard bump.

This is not, I think, how our life of faith should be. It reflects a dividing line in our reality which should be integrated as one. It can feel comforting, when we are going through our personal moments of crisis, to find ourselves in a space where we can lay those burdens down. This is valuable and essential for many of us. But it is also important that collectively we find ways to close the gap between faith and the burdens that face us as a human family. Without this, we can, even accidentally, begin to preach, pray and speak as if reality is divided. We might read that 'God so loved the world' (John 3:16), but in reality we act as if 'God so loved the church'. The church and its concerns become the priority, and 'the world' is demonised or left to itself.

Something has gone awry in contexts where, as Christians, we seek to be detached from 'the world' because we imagine we are pure and others are fundamentally impure. In this binary way of thinking, the Church is presumed to be a place that is fundamentally good, where people are trustworthy and where we will experience God. 'The world' is an evil place, where everything and everyone must be treated with suspicion and is presumed to be godless. We are encouraged to lay our guard down in the Church but to build huge walls to protect ourselves from 'the world'. Yet, in reality, our churches can be slow to demonstrate the love, gentleness, patience and righteousness that are said to be fruits of the Spirit (see Galatians 5:22–3). Some people who do not declare faith in God at all can offer some of the best examples of fighting for justice and peace, truth and love in the world.

The divide that can exist in our collective mind between the sacred and the secular, the spiritual and the material, the Church and the world, can shape all of our church traditions in particular ways. Often, it leads to disengagement, pride and self-righteousness on our part. Integrating our lives of faith – individually and collectively – with what is happening in the wider world is, I believe, important for the robustness of our own faithfulness to

God and our witness to the gospel. This does not mean conforming to everything we see, but recognising that the Spirit of God is interested in engaging with the world that God so loves. If we are willing, we might get to play a part in the work God is doing in creation as a whole.

## Questions for reflection

1 What stands out for you as you think about the people, churches and contexts that have shaped your understanding of reality?

2 To what extent do you resonate with the idea that we can often live in what feels like two different worlds as people of faith?

3 Have you found ways to integrate your faith with the whole of your life beyond the time you spend at church? If so, what are some of the ways in which you do this? If not, what is challenging for you?

# Dualism problems

For many, our Christianity has been shaped by Western philosophical norms even though we do not realise it. As a result, it can be difficult to hold an integrated worldview that does not put what we consider 'spiritual' above what we think of as 'natural' or 'material'. Viewing reality as a conflict between two different elements is a very particular way of seeing things that is not common to all global cultures. If we want to trace where these thoughts started, we can go back to Plato, the ancient Greek philosopher who died around three hundred years before Jesus. Plato is known for thinking about reality in terms of dualisms, and his thoughts influenced the Greco-Roman world into which Christianity was born.

By dualisms, I mean that Plato played with the idea that reality comprised various aspects in tension or conflict, usually with one being better. So, for example, there is in his thought a material, tangible world that is temporary and of which we need to let go, and a higher, greater reality that we need to reach for. Another dualism for Plato was the idea that being human involved a conflict between the soul and the body. The body, which is material and temporary, has desires and hungers of various kinds. The body is the lower part of the self, the base self, and it must be restrained and disciplined. The soul is immortal, it is interested in higher things and is the part of ourselves we must be led by. As we read in one of Plato's dialogues, *Phaedo*:

> It is clear first of all in the case of physical pleasures that the philosopher frees his soul from the association with the body, so far as is possible, to a greater extent than other men? ... When it [the soul] tries to investigate anything with the help of the body, it is obviously led astray ... Surely the soul can best reflect when it is free of all distractions such as hearing or

sight or pain or pleasure of any kind – that is, when it ignores the body and becomes as far as possible independent, avoiding all physical contacts and associations as much as it can, in search of reality.[1]

This small part of Plato's thought might not seem important, but it is when we consider the implications this can have for our beliefs and how we live. We can see from this description the potential connections with Christian beliefs about the life of faith. People debate the extent to which Plato's thought has influenced Christian theology, especially Paul, and this is one example where the comparison is quite stark. Paul's letter to the Romans is full of language which conveys the idea that there is a battle that goes on within our own selves. There is something about us, in his mind, that is destructive and needs to be managed, or in even stronger terms, 'put to death' (Romans 8:13). But simultaneously, he explains that 'life and peace' are present within us through the Spirit, who shapes how we think and leads us away from anything that undermines our life with God and others (Romans 8:6). There is quite a lot of overlap, at least on the surface, between Plato's ideas and Paul's notion of living 'according to the flesh' or 'according to the Spirit' (Romans 8:4–5). It can be a helpful way of explaining our experiences and the life of faith. But every analogy has limits, and without the balance of other images or metaphors, we can end up in some unhelpful places.

It is not hard to see how the idea that the body and soul are in conflict could contribute to Christian theologies that tell us we must suppress and control the body (and the bodies of others) in order to attain spiritual virtues. If the body is a problem, then it can follow (at least in some people's minds) that we must punish it, deprive it and force it into submission – and expect others to do the same with theirs. Sometimes we might not go this far – we may just have a view that our spiritual lives are the most important aspect of ourselves. As a result, we might, even unknowingly, neglect our emotional, mental, psychological or physical well-being. We might look down on those who prioritise aspects of their lives we would consider to be less 'spiritual' or godly, such as relationships and rest. Within this way of thinking, depriving the body and everything concerned with it is considered the path to spiritual freedom and to God.

But the logic can be taken in an even more destructive direction. If the body is simply an unimportant outer casing for the person who at their core is a spirit or soul, then what we do to bodies ceases to matter. This kind of dualism leaves the door open for us to abuse our own bodies or those of others, since the emphasis is on what we do to the soul or spirit. Within this dualistic perspective, it is possible to abuse a person physically while claiming to care for their soul or spiritual well-being. You can keep a person's body in chains and simultaneously claim to offer them spiritual freedom.

This has been one of the ongoing questions that womanist (Black feminist), Black, postcolonial and feminist theologies have sought to address: how do we prevent this breakdown? Haunted by the question of how white Christians in the American South could go along to watch a Black person be lynched (chased by a mob, beaten and hung in a tree until dead), womanist theologian Kelly Brown Douglas holds Plato's influence on Christianity responsible:

In the American theological scene, platonized Christianity perhaps found its most comfortable home in the evangelical Protestant tradition. This was the prominent tradition of the American South. This was the tradition that most significantly shaped the theological consciousness of those whites who were party to Black lynchings. This same tradition, ironically, was also the tradition to which many early Black Christians in America were converted. In this regard, platonized

Christianity has had an impact on Black lives not simply in the ways in which the Black body has been subjugated by white culture, but also in the ways that platonized views have been integrated into the Black faith tradition.[2]

This is one of the great flaws in the theology that many of us have inherited, regardless of our race. It has done harm to all of us, whether or not we identify with those who have suffered. Many of us have been taught to divide our reality – and even ourselves – down the middle, seeing some aspects as important and others as less so. Our emotions, our minds and our embodied experiences are all considered secondary when we believe that our spiritual selves are the most important. This dualism also invites us to pridefully categorise ourselves and others as 'good' or 'bad', 'holy' or 'unholy', 'saved' or 'unsaved', as if we know what is in our own hearts and those of others. Ironically, our connection to God, as well as our relationship with ourselves, others and the natural world, all suffer when we think of reality in this way.

This dualistic view has ended up having a significantly negative impact, because often those of us who have inherited these perspectives have nothing to act as a counterbalance. Global perspectives in faith, spirituality and philosophy enable us to locate correctives to ensure we do not go too far. The majority of our global population do not emphasise dualisms and divides in discussions of our reality. In contrast, the emphasis tends to be on the interconnectedness and interdependence of all things. Rather than trying to force reality into set boxes that are in conflict, there is space for creativity, fluidity and surprise. Traditional African beliefs offer us examples of such perspectives.

## Embracing the body: African spirituality

African cultures offer some important contributions to Christian faith, theology and spirituality. This includes the embrace of embodied experience and expression, a holistic view of reality and openness to the Spirit and the spiritual. In explaining these aspects of African spirituality and faith, I do not mean to suggest that those who do not have African heritage do not share them. Embodied expression in worship can be very diverse: kneeling to pray, walking up to receive Holy Communion, dancing in the aisle of a church and so on.

No spirituality or culture has a monopoly on the body. But I do want to give special attention to how traditional African religions and worldviews enhance Christian faith and spirituality for all people. This is especially to counteract any notion that what is traditionally African is assumed to be anti-Christian and even demonic. In traditional Yoruba religion, for example, the body is understood to be core to the act of worship. Worship includes the body in dancing, lying prostrate, shouting and group movement. The body is not a problem for worship, but essential to it. Harvey Kwiyani, the mission theologian from Malawi, puts it this way: 'Be it in trances and spirit possession, or in lifting up holy hands or dancing in the church, the spirit and the body are constantly influencing one another. The body is not an enemy to the spirit.'[3]

While restricting the body's movement might be considered essential to church services within some white European settings, the opposite is true for Africans. The body, vibrant music and dance are not a distraction from worship, even if they may be considered to be such elsewhere. What we feel and sense with our bodies becomes a sign of our spirituality, not something to be suppressed. Encounter with God is expected to be *felt*. To speak about God being 'here' opens up the possibility that we might feel God with our actual senses. How could it be that God, the source of life, who made us and knows us (including our bodies), might be among us, and yet we would not *feel* it? The thought is almost absurd. This feeling may be a tingle in the fingertips, a wave of emotion, an urge to dance or shout, butterflies in the stomach or an internal sense of peace or joy in prayer. It is different for each person.

This hope for an embodied personal experience of God is underpinned by the expectation that God meets us in all aspects of our lives, and encounter with God is holistic. If we return again to traditional African beliefs, we find a common expectation that encounters with the divine can take place anywhere. In fact, spaces such as the marketplace, which we might consider to be secular spaces, are prime sites for encounters with spiritual powers. While there are still sacred spaces where religious rituals, worship and events take place, this does not mean other spaces are 'secular'; all of life is recognised as spiritual. Spiritual realities can affect us anywhere, whether for good or bad, as the Revd Chigor Chike explains:

> It is quite common among Africans to trace the root causes of a misfortune such as a road accident or an illness to such spiritual things as one's relationship with one's ancestors or the actions of deities or evil spirits ... This acute awareness of the spiritual nature of the world is one of the main reasons why Africans are very religious ... religion can be seen as the indigenous African way of living in harmony with the spiritual forces that surround them.[4]

Recognising the spiritual in all aspects of life, rather than thinking of the spiritual as attached only to sacred places, opens up the possibilities for faith to have something to offer all the elements of our existence. It offers an all-encompassing vision of God's presence that is not limited to particular aspects of our reality.

There are, of course, risks with this perspective, which is why all cultural viewpoints must learn from one another. It is easy to see how interpreting all events as spiritual might undermine the importance of human action. If the cause of socio-economic disadvantage is 'the spirit of poverty', then why bother scrutinising the impact of government policy? Can we pray poverty away if an evil spirit is the cause? Important questions have to be asked of African-rooted theologies, as with all theologies, in order to draw the best out of them for the sake of the Church and the world, while addressing any limitations.

Overall, this openness to the spiritual and the valuing of our tangible, material lives is a good balance to dualistic ideas. When life is understood as one interconnected reality, in which God meets us, we might be open to God's voice and guidance even in places considered 'secular'. We recognise that there are aspects of our reality that we cannot see and understand. And we become open to those mystical elements of our faith that we cannot always explain with words.

Not all of us are familiar with this kind of holistic view of reality or spirituality, but it is good for us to reflect on the assumptions we might make about where we might learn about and experience God. For many people, the church is the space where they are able to gather together for worship and expect to grow in faith. There are some activities and traditions that revolve around particular dedicated spaces in church buildings, such as an altar for the Eucharist. There are important theological reasons why they exist, and they do not necessarily undermine a holistic view of spirituality. The use of bread 'that human hands have made'[5] points to the embrace of the material or tangible within church-centred events.

But the church can be a challenging space for many people, for different reasons. Some, especially those who are neurodiverse, struggle to listen to and focus on services that depend on particular rhythms and styles. Others find church to be restrictive, and they learn and explore faith better through discussions and other activities in which they can participate, rather than listening to a preacher or singing words that others decide for them. Embracing the body and the various ways our bodies can be involved in worship opens up opportunities for all of us, especially those we often forget, to belong even more in our communities of faith.

## Questions for reflection

1 In what ways is your own faith or spiritual practice affected by dualistic perspectives?
2 How does, or how might, a more holistic view of yourself as a person change the way you reflect, pray and respond to yourself and to others?
3 How might a broader understanding of the 'sacred' enhance the life and spiritual practice of your faith community?

# Embodying faith

The willingness to explore important and sometimes difficult questions is at the core of the Christian life as well as the work of theology. My questioning began as a young teenager, even if later as a theologian I would find ways to explore my big questions in a more organised and committed way. These questions were born out of my experience as a young Black girl growing up in a loving family and church, and in the inner city, where people were often just scraping by, struggling with low-paid jobs and a lack of opportunities. In this context, I was taught that faith was a matter of what we believed *and* what we did with our bodies, especially in relation to others. Faith was something we developed as we read the Bible, were filled with the Spirit and followed the example of those around us who were more mature in the faith. We did not imagine that it was important to write down our beliefs, but rather that we lived them.

Black spiritualities are sometimes viewed as inferior because of this emphasis on practice. Many histories, philosophies and theologies have been passed down in oral tradition from generation to generation. This makes preaching and testimony an important part of Black Christian life for many. Preaching itself, though the sermon is prepared usually by one person, is a communal moment. The hearty 'amens' and 'hallelujahs' are the hearers affirming that what the preacher is saying is true, based on what they know from their own lived experience and from Scripture. It is a way of cheering the preacher on and encouraging them to dig even more deeply in their reflections, many of which will be spontaneous and not prepared in advance. As Carol Tomlin explains:

> In call–response, the audience or congregants respond to the preacher who, in turn, shapes his or her homily according to the audience's response. A favourable response will encourage the preacher to continue in the same or similar vein in their

discourse; conversely, a muted response may suggest a change of course in the direction of the sermon or the implementation of new strategies to engage the audience. The interaction of the preacher and congregants is a highly sensitive one and indeed a symbiotic relationship. Such a symbiotic relationship depends to a large extent on shared experiences, core values and insight of biblical texts based on group solidarity.[1]

Preaching is an essential space, where theologies are passed on, teaching takes place and people's spiritual lives are nurtured. In contexts where English is a second language, sermons can be punctuated with multiple languages or dialects very easily. For people who do not have access to the latest technology, preaching is an accessible way to share with a whole community. It is an inclusive avenue for sharing theological and spiritual knowledge. Black communities have not always prioritised writing down this knowledge, though this is changing. When intellectual reasoning and written arguments are celebrated as the most important ways of knowing and sharing knowledge, it is easy to see why those who use other strategies might be considered less capable or less intelligent. This, of course, is not the case.

African figures have provided us with essential writings that have helped us to understand God from the earliest days of the Church. I am not suggesting here that the forms of Christianity that emerge from Black communities are anti-intellectual. Tertullian, Athanasius, Augustine, Origen and others were African men who critically engaged with the Scriptures and Tradition to lay out guidelines for the Church. Black theologians and writers continue to do important work in articulating the embodied faith of Black communities. Theology is indeed something African people do.

Yet it is also the case that, in the context of Black faith, there can be some suspicion when there is a very strong focus on debating doctrine and little or none on how we live in the light of the Scriptures – what we might call ethics. This is in part, I think, because Black people, along with others, have felt all too well the limitations of a faith that is concerned with defending right doctrine (orthodoxy) but is not interested in examining the impact of faith on lived experience (orthopraxy). Historically, one could be aligned with Christian orthodoxy and also be an owner of and trader in African human beings, or steal land from and murder indigenous people. Settling the debates about whether the Spirit proceeded from the Father and the Son, or whether the Son was created, did not mean Christians knew better how to love those in front of their eyes. Christian orthodoxy has often failed to prevent Christian violence in practice, even if the theory is readily available. Contemporary Black theologians and believers, as a result, have developed a deep concern for being doers and not only hearers of the word, for neighbour love as well as the love of God.

This was drilled into me as a child. We were the kind of family who had Bible studies at home. My dad had a huge Bible, which we called 'the Moses Bible' because we imagined it weighed as much as the stone tablets Moses carried down from Mount Sinai. We would often sit around the table talking during and after dinner, and a few times a month Dad would take the Bible out of the cabinet and find a passage for us to read. It was usually something my dad or mum had been reading in their morning devotion, and we would pass the Bible around (almost spraining our arms) and take turns to read it aloud. Dad would ask us to choose our key verse, the one that stood out to us as capturing the essence of the passage we had just read. We never ended these times without asking what it meant for how we were supposed to live our lives.

My parents had learnt from their parents that, while we might not be able to get our head around the Trinity or how exactly to understand the power of God in a wildly unfair world, we were responsible for living right. Living right did not require a BA, an MA or a PhD in theology, biblical studies or anything else. Living right was a matter of the heart. It was the essence of what it meant to be a Christian. Living right was, in my parents' view, linked to very clear guidelines for behaviour. It meant being careful how you treat people, whether or not they are considered important in the eyes of the world and whether or not anyone else was watching – because God was. It meant being careful about what went into your mouth and what came out: a little alcohol was okay, but swearing, gossip and rudeness were never allowed. It meant having an appropriate relationship with your money, recognising it as a tool but not worshipping it, and always paying your tithes and offerings. It meant respecting your parents, being kind to one another and helping out a neighbour in need.

This clear understanding of the Christian life was rooted in the person of Jesus and his ways of being in the world. Jesus, as God enfleshed, is the central figure for those of us who call ourselves Christians. He is the one who is understood to show us God the Father, and who promised us the Holy Spirit who now abides with us. Jesus is particularly important because, in his incarnation, he embraced the body when he took on flesh to dwell among us.

The incarnation is one of the most fascinating aspects of Christian faith – the idea that God would become a human being in order to be known to us. That Christ, who existed at the beginning, would take on human form in order to draw us into right relationship with God and all God has made. Jesus himself bypasses the binary thinking that requires people to choose between two ways of being. He is both fully human and fully divine, bringing together in one what is considered irreconcilable. Womanist theologian Eboni Marshall Turman calls Jesus' body 'unorthodox' because of its hosting of two realities that have been considered to be in conflict.[2]

In Jesus, the body is not unimportant, dirty, evil or suspicious. The incarnation reminds us that humanity (including human bodies) is created 'very good', just like God said in Genesis 1:31. But there is an additional aspect to Jesus' embodiment which has been highlighted by Black theologians as important for all who experience various forms of struggle in this life: the particular flesh that Jesus chose to inhabit. African American mystic Howard Thurman explains that, as a poor Jew living under Roman occupation, Jesus' life was aligned with those 'whose backs are against the wall'. The majority of people in the world fit into this category, he says, caught up in systems, cultures and structures that mean they are exploited and often rendered powerless. He explains it this way:

> The economic predicament with which [Jesus] was identified in birth placed him initially with the great mass of [people] on the earth. The masses of the people are poor. If we dare take the position that in Jesus there was at work some radical destiny, it would be safe to say that in his poverty he was more truly Son of man than he would have been if the incident of family or birth had made him a rich son of Israel.[3]

For Thurman, whose spiritual writings were born out of a context in which African peoples were enslaved, then systematically condemned to poverty, Jesus is a friend who stands in solidarity with them. In the midst of untold troubles, the weight of oppressive socio-economic systems and the burdens of racism, Jesus appears as one who understands. Jesus is a 'Black hero', in the words of Anthony Reddie.[4] In various global contexts, people have come to know God in these ways, and have been empowered by these perspectives. While for some, Jesus may be known only as a king or a lord who remains distant and aloof, for those 'whose backs are against the wall', Jesus is a friend who is 'closer than a brother' (Proverbs 18:24). He is familiar with what they endure and what they suffer, and is trusted to be their advocate.

## Reconciling all things

Colossians 1 includes one of my favourite passages in Scripture, and it is one that is important for our discussion of the oneness of all things in

Christian faith and African experience. It begins with an encouraging greeting to the faithful believers, where the writer declares aloud his prayers for those who will come to read it. The writer then launches into what has become known as the hymn of or to Christ:

> The Son is the image of the invisible God, the firstborn over all creation. For in him all things were created: things in heaven and on earth, visible and invisible, whether thrones or powers or rulers or authorities; all things have been created through him and for him. He is before all things, and in him all things hold together. And he is the head of the body, the church; he is the beginning and the firstborn from among the dead, so that in everything he might have the supremacy. For God was pleased to have all his fullness dwell in him, and through him to reconcile to himself all things, whether things on earth or things in heaven.
> (Colossians 1:15–20)

This understanding of Christ and creation can offer an antidote to a dualistic way of thinking that can undermine a holistic faith. Categorising reality into opposing types, and elevating some as more important, can prevent us from experiencing the abundant life Jesus spoke about with his disciples. This abundance was about a life filled to the brim with God's Spirit, and being led to serve God and others, as seen in the example of Christ. Holistic faith gets into every corner of our lives, and brings to life and wholeness every aspect of *who* we are and *how* we are in the world. In this passage, we see this wholeness emphasised in the repetition of 'all'. This passage offers us a way of seeing reality, all we know, all that exists, has existed and will exist, as born from the one source, Christ. All things are created by one, through one and for one.

It is this oneness that should, I think, shape our understanding of God, of ourselves, of the Church and of creation as a whole. God is one, and the Son is the fullness of the one God in front of our eyes. There is no conflict in Jesus, though he holds together within himself all of God and the fullness of humanity. He embodies wholeness in his very self, and from this point moves through his context at one with God. He is deeply connected with those he encounters and with the context in which he lives. He is fully present in those moments, so much so that he can spot the person bent over and hovering at the back of the synagogue who is in need of his healing. He notices the person on the edge whom others miss, and the person who is hiding in a tree. But Jesus Christ also exhibits a timelessness: he was before all things, even though we read about his birth in flesh. He was seated at the beginning in the darkness, as the Spirit hovered over the waters, and declared, 'Let us make human beings in our image' (Genesis 1:26 NLT).

To understand our lives as created beings in the light of this passage in Colossians is to recognise our place among 'all things'. We can often think ourselves as humanity to be very special, more so than the natural world, for example. And this can mean that we elevate ourselves in ways that are detrimental to our relationship with the rest of creation. This passage calls us to remember that, as a whole, we as human beings are part of a creation that we do not own and did not order. This is despite the destructive impact and disorder we often bring about. We are part of 'all things' made by and for Christ, and are held together by Christ, who is also reconciling all of creation with God. Christ is, as Rowan Williams describes, 'the heart of creation':

> From our point of view in the universe as we experience it, creation is at its optimal level of action and well-being when finite love and intelligence are in accord with the uncreated love and intelligence that the Word eternally exercises. This is the sense in which Jesus Christ is at the heart of creation – or the apex of creation, depending on our basic imagery – as the

one in whom the movement or energy of eternal filial love and understanding is fully active in and as finite substance and agency. From the created point of view (the only one we can occupy, needless to say), the best we can say unaided about God is that God is that *in* which everything finds coherence and *on* which all acts converge (material or immaterial).[5]

The Church, which is the body of Christ, is one not through an act of the human will but because of the work of Christ who is her head. Christ existed before the Church, created the Church and holds the Church together. This is not about a particular denomination or tradition being created and held together by God. Individual churches have been created by men and women in boardrooms and front rooms, and they have died down and died out, and they will again. But Christ, through the work of his Spirit, has drawn and is drawing people into his body by grace, through faith. This Church includes those who cannot gather because of persecution, or because of a particular church's refusal to make space or ramps or to otherwise remove barriers. This body cannot be counted, controlled or predetermined by violence, vision meetings or strategic planning. It does not belong to us, but we are 'grafted in' (Romans 11:17–19, 23–4). It includes those we would rather not have as part of the same body as us. This work of God cannot be undermined, voted down or destroyed by human hands, nor by 'the gates of Hades' (Matthew 16:18). It is Christ who is the head of this body and Christ who sustains it, in all its various forms and in all the places and times it appears.

As we tarry with this idea of the oneness of all things, which is rooted in the oneness of God, many thoughts and feelings can arise. We might be reminded of the gap between what we read in the Scriptures and believe, and what we see. This can be deeply disheartening. In speaking of the oneness of all things in Christ, I am not denying the divisions and hierarchies that characterise our life together. I will get to many of them in the subsequent chapters. But I want to begin with this foundational thought that is both deeply African and inherent to Black cultures, and also fundamentally Christian.

To speak of oneness is not to speak of sameness, but of the fundamental interdependence and interconnectedness of all creation, which finds its source in God. This is a joyous truth, that my life is bound together with yours, and with all peoples and with all of creation, despite the fact that, in reality, this can mean we might suffer undue pain and oppression when others withhold good from us or do us harm. Our frustration at this gap between the truth and the reality is an indication, I think, that we know deep down that things should not be this way. The longing we have for right relationships between all people, dignity for all and justice for the oppressed is born from this knowledge, which we cannot always articulate.

I mentioned the Eucharist earlier and want to give it a little more attention here, in thinking about the oneness of the Church and the oneness of all things. To be invited around the Lord's table is a privilege that none of us deserves. As we gather around the table that is not our own, at which we are guests, we are reminded, as I stated above, that we do not own the Church either. It is an important sacrament, reminding us of the reconciling work of Christ even while we tarry for this reconciliation in our experience. Of course, we experience moments of this reconciliation in the meantime. We find a friendship can be salvaged after all; we experience a community that celebrates all people regardless of race, class, gender or sexuality; we discover that love can be restored between a parent and a long-lost child; or a person comes to faith again. Our hope is built up by these moments.

The Eucharist, I believe, is also supposed to be such a moment. It is a time when we accept a gift that tells us a truth that even we might like to deny: that we are all children of God and siblings of one another. We are reminded that it is through Christ's life, death and resurrection that we have been reconciled to God and to one another. But we might take this even further. Theologian M. Shawn Copeland asks us to imagine what it means for us to live in light of the Eucharist as Christ's body in a world in which certain bodies experience oppression and harm:

> Our daily living out, and out of the dangerous memory of the torture and abuse, death and resurrection of Jesus Christ constitutes us as his own body raised up and made visible in the world. As his *body*, we embrace with love and hope those who, in their bodies, are despised and even marginalised, even as we embrace with love and forgiveness those whose sins spawn the conditions for the suffering and oppression of others. As *his body* we pulse with new life, for Eucharist is the heart of Christian community ... Eucharistic solidarity is a virtue, a practice of cognitive and bodily commitments oriented to meet the social consequences of Eucharist. We [human beings] strive to become what we have received and do what we are being made.[6]

Here, the Eucharist transcends every division in time, in place and within or between people. The Eucharistic moment erases every dualism and dividing line, bringing all things together. The memory of what has passed is viewed through the lens of the present gathering. And the moment of gathering is reflective of the future that awaits all of creation. So we are joined together in this Holy Communion with the saints who have gone before us, and with those who stand with us in the moment we wait to receive the bread and the wine. So also will we be joined with all those who receive this meal in all places around the world, and with those who will do so after we have taken our final breath. And we are called to this table from every background, language, identity and group, to feast on the one who is the source of our life. And then to live out this truth, in our day-to-day lives, as we make friends, buy our groceries, share meals and travel to work. We embody this 'Eucharistic solidarity', as Copeland calls it, as we remain mindful of the bodies that are absent, or harmed in some way by the sins of others, and of our socio-economic, political and cultural life. This is something we strive for, even as we recognise that we cannot do it in our own strength, but only by the grace of the one who calls us by name, and to whom we will give an account.

## Questions for reflection

1 To what extent does reconciliation feature in how you imagine God to be present and bringing life to creation?
2 What needs to be reconciled within yourself, in your church or community and in the world at large? How do we tarry well for this reconciliation?
3 In your experience of the Eucharist, do you feel aware of what Copeland calls its 'social consequences' as well as its spiritual importance? What might this contribute to your understanding of this sacrament?

# 3

# Movement

Movement is one of the most constant aspects of life. Whether or not we want to, we move through time and we move through space. Each of our individual lives begins with movement. As time passes, we go from being tiny, undetectable cells to a whole human being, all the various aspects of our bodies and minds having been formed. We leave the comfort of our mother's womb, moving into the world with our first breath and a cry to open up our lungs. We are, as children, moved from here to there in the arms of those who care for us. We are carried into the car, or to bed, and, for most of us, we then find our way to moving all on our own. We might waddle around on our legs, clinging to the edges of chairs and tables to get to where we need to go. Or we figure out how to use various aids to help us to get around in the world. We learn to explore and we grow in confidence, enjoying the freedom of getting exactly where we saw ourselves being. Before long, many of us will venture outside, first with those tasked with our safety, and eventually alone. We will take our first journey to school, or into town to see friends, or to the park or local shops. Soon the world will be our oyster.

Maybe. Movement is a privilege. Having the option of where to go, when and with whom helps to make up what many of us would consider to be a good quality of life. This is well known, of course, by those who live with long-term health issues or disabilities and do not have the support needed to venture out when they want to. It will also be familiar to those who have ever sought to enter, return or remain in a country that treats them with suspicion because of their particular passport or status.

All of us are likely to have become more aware of this when our movements were restricted during the Covid-19 pandemic. We were not free to travel and move around our neighbourhood, city, country or the world at will. We were forced to stay at home unless we worked in one of those indispensable jobs that looked after everyone's health or ensured people could have access to food and other essential items. This temporary restriction may have been something of a haven for you if, like me, you find yourself on the more introverted end of the personality spectrum. But even for us, the lack of freedom to move around may have begun to wear down our sense of contentment.

Having said this, moving back out into the world after Covid restrictions were relaxed felt like a challenge and was even fear-inducing. This continues to be acute for those of us who are immuno-compromised and risk complications to pre-existing conditions. Yet even for those without additional health worries, returning to pre-Covid patterns has taken some getting used to. This is because, whether or not we always recognise it, movement can demand a lot from us. Movement involves leaving what is comfortable and familiar to enter into a new space. Even if what is familiar is not that great, it still feels safe to some extent because we know what to expect.

Some of us spent months only interacting in person with a handful of people, they became hyper-familiar to us. We could predict their tone, meaning, reactions and expressions. At the same time, everyone else became like strangers. Being around people we had known for years, even, suddenly became awkward. Our ability to engage in small talk declined – maybe we could no longer remember to manage our facial expressions or body language. We had to learn again how to interact positively with others, and how to interpret the behaviours of other people. Movement requires energy.

Movement is not only a reality that we all experience as individuals in the course of our lives, but it can also affect whole groups of people. Movement is not only a journey I take, but also something we experience together. It is a core element of Black life and thus Black faith and spirituality. Movement can be forced, and it can be chosen. It can occur as a combination of external factors and internal motivation. It can involve a journey to a known destination or to somewhere yet to be discovered.

Movement can also be a combination of physical change and spiritual transformation. The Scriptures offer us many examples of movement, as people search for a new life and wait for the fulfilment of the promise they have received from God. Movement is therefore essential to tarrying. To tarry does not always mean to be still – we can wait for God even while we move. We can move towards a promised future, even as we await its fulfilment and the intervention of God.

As we reflect on movement in this chapter, consider how movement, or lack of movement, has shaped and is currently shaping your life. This might be movement in relation to countries or continents, in relation to your home or work, or it might trigger reflections on shifts happening or needing to happen within your mind and heart during this time.

## Abraham: A model for movement?

My grandad Selvin considers himself a contemporary Abraham. Not in the sense that he should be considered a patriarch of the faith – though many who know him well would consider him a spiritual father – but because of their shared histories of movement and migration.

My grandad quotes the Bible at every opportunity. The Bible is so much a part of his language that, without thinking, he draws on it to answer the most mundane questions or make random comments. The Bible is the book my grandad knows more than anything else; it seeps out in his everyday speech, even in his jokes.

This was not always the case. My grandad grew up in a family that was not Christian. On occasions, we encourage him to remember his former self and tell us stories of his younger years of mischief, drinking and smoking. But mostly he likes to pretend he has always been the sanctified Pentecostal who does not defile himself with the 'things of the flesh'. Unlike his old social habits, which have all disappeared, thankfully his sense of humour has remained intact, though it has taken on a much more biblical flavour. He has not infrequently called himself 'a lamb led to slaughter' when we are returning his teasing and banter. He is not as innocent as Jesus by any stretch, but Bible humour is one of his favourites.

If you are lucky enough to have or to have had kind grandparents with whom you have had the chance to spend time, you will hopefully have had opportunities to hear their stories. My grandad Selvin and my nan Brynel lived twenty-five minutes from our house as I grew up, so we would often see them. My grandad's favourite story to tell is about his awe at how his life has turned out. Usually, I can tell the story is coming. He will be sitting in his comfy chair in his bedroom, which is downstairs in my auntie's house. His legs don't move like they used to, and neither do his fingers, so he needs a lot more help to do things. I will be sitting on the bed, chatting with him, or maybe we will be watching a rerun of *Columbo* (one of the best things he has given me is an appreciation of this dishevelled TV detective).

As we sit, various of my cousins will pop their heads around the door. Maybe even one of his great-grandchildren will push open the door and waddle in with someone behind them, ready to catch them if they should lose their balance. And my grandad will look at them, and chuckle in his warm voice, and his eyes will fill with pride. And he will look across at me and begin: 'Sel, my cyan' believe dat is me one come a Inglan' wid five poun inna mi pocket, an luk ya.' My grandad will then explain how he arrived in England alone, prayerful and hopeful, to find work, and would eventually send for my nan and some of their children. My oldest uncle was left with a relative and came over in his early teenage years.

My grandad will go on to speak about the challenges of those early years in England. He traded many treasures. The warmth of the Jamaican sunshine, luscious greenery and otherworldly beaches were replaced by snow, rain and concrete. Working in the fresh air with his hands in the soil, alongside his family, was a distant memory as he laboured in a smoky, sweltering foundry alongside sometimes hostile strangers. He will explain the difficulty of losing his job and trying to feed seven children on insufficient money. He might even shed a tear at this memory. And then he will speak about how he would pray, and sometimes a bag of food would appear on the doorstep. His countenance will change as he recalls how they made it through.

He will speak about the number of his descendants. And then he will draw on the story of Abraham: 'The Lord called Abraham,' he will say as he starts his bedroom sermon, 'and told him he would bring him into a strange land.' This is his story too. 'He told Abraham that he would have more descendants than grains of sand!' This is not quite true of my grandad, of course, but seven children, fourteen grandchildren and four great-grandchildren isn't bad. My grandad will tell me, as he always does, that he prays every day for each of us by name. His story is one of determination, prayerfulness and the grace of God.

My grandad is a theological genius, though he has never written down a word. His reflections would, in another life, have earned him a professorial role in one of the most renowned universities in the world. The connection he has made between the story of Abraham and his own journey of movement is, I think, essential for any consideration of Black spirituality and faith.

Abraham is a figure important to multiple religions, of course. For Muslims, Jewish communities and Christians across the breadth of traditions, he is recognised as a spiritual forefather. As a lover of history and adventure stories, I have always been captivated by the early stories in Genesis, including that of Abraham (first called Abram). He is minding his own business when he hears the call to leave everything he knows to travel to a land God will show him. God promises to bless, provide for and multiply Abraham so that he will become a great nation that will bless the peoples of the whole earth (Genesis 12:1–3). Abraham moves in obedience from what is familiar to follow a God he does not yet know. So begins a story of migration and travel for generations. Abraham and Sarah's descendants are a people on the move.

There are some important points to make about this story. The story of Abraham has been co-opted in many different contexts and used for violent purposes, which we must recognise. This is the challenge of reading the Bible – it does not come with a manual that explains, 'This is how to use and *not* to use this passage.' This is, of course, what keeps people like me in a job.

As the story unfolds, we find that this promise that Abraham will become a great nation leads to the rape of Hagar, an enslaved African woman from Egypt. Sarah, desperate for her own progress, treats Hagar as collateral damage. She comes up with a plan to force Hagar to be a surrogate for the promised child of her and her husband. Delores Williams has famously spoken of Hagar as a person of great significance for African American women who were sexually exploited as forced surrogates throughout slavery. She explains the similarities:

Hagar was brutalized by her slave owner, the Hebrew woman Sarah … Hagar had no control over her body. It belonged to her slave owner, whose husband, Abraham, ravished Hagar. A child Ishmael was born; mother and child were eventually cast out of Abraham's and Sarah's home without resources for survival … Time after time [African slave women] were raped by their owners and bore children whom the masters seldom claimed … Hagar resisted the brutalities of slavery by running away. Black American women have a long resistance history that includes running away from slavery ... But [Hagar] had serious personal and salvific encounters with God – encounters which aided Hagar in the survival struggle of herself and her son. Over and over again, Black women in the churches have testified about their serious personal and salvific encounters with God, encounters that helped them and their families survive.[1]

There is no sisterhood between Sarah and Hagar. There is only the one who makes decisions and the one who bears the consequences. Women from communities around the world have known and continue to know intimately the trauma of labour and sexual exploitation. We cannot forget those who, even today, are trafficked and live under the yoke of slavery. Too many of God's children know what it is to be treated as an object and a 'thing' – even by those who claim to be working towards God's promised future. Later on, as Abraham and Sarah's descendants move into the land they believe is theirs by divine right, we see tale after tale of genocide and mass murder. Whole peoples are wiped out so they can have room to be a great nation. These texts have been used historically by Europeans and others who believed themselves to be God's great people and sought to legitimise the abuse, dehumanisation and murder of people they considered to be 'heathens'.

It is also important to say that the reasons for Abraham's movement are very different from those that caused my grandad to leave his home in Jamaica. For Abraham, who as far as we know was living relatively comfortably, the only motivation was a somewhat random call from an unknown God. For my grandad, as is the case with many who migrate from their homelands, the choice to leave was much more complicated. My grandparents' generation of African Caribbeans were British citizens but located abroad. Britain's Empire made Black and brown people British. So their move from Jamaica to the UK was simply an extended version of taking a flight from Belfast to Birmingham. This is an especially fitting comparison, since Ireland was the first place to be colonised by England. English people have also often treated Irish people as 'foreign' and inferior. 'No Blacks, no dogs, no Irish' was the infamous wording painted or pinned to various houses and establishments during the 1960s.

Moving to the UK was necessary for my grandparents, owing to the lack of opportunities in Jamaica, an island still gasping for breath in the aftermath of its history of slavery and colonialism. They also moved in response to the request for workers to rebuild post-war Britain. If they had felt that viable options existed for them to remain in Jamaica and build their lives as they hoped, they most definitely would have stayed – and many did. This, of course, is the case for the majority of those on the move today.

Certain bodies are pushed and pulled, first this way and then that. But Abraham is invited to go. I think this is why my grandad resonates with this story. Not that the British government's call should be understood as God's call in his story, but my grandad made an active choice to leave while others stayed.

I always read God's words as invitations in the Scriptures, since this is what I see in the person of Jesus. Even when the word 'command' is used by the writers, I hear it as an invitation. So, when God tells Abraham to 'Go from … your father's household,' I am clear in my mind that Abraham could have said no. That 'no' would not have meant he was cursed, simply that he would have missed out on an adventure.

The conversations between God and Abraham read like a dialogue between two parties; there is no domination here. We even find what looks like a debate about God's destruction of Sodom in Genesis 18:16–33. It appears that these two friends go back and forth, and God in the end goes along with what Abraham suggests. Imagine that! I wonder whether God had spoken to others and they had politely declined. Abraham, though, was curious enough to say, 'I will.'

And so the adventure begins. It is a journey that will involve twists and turns. It will be so challenging he may wonder whether he should have even started. This is very much the story of my paternal grandparents. I don't think they imagined they would have to face what they did. They expected the population to be prepared, they expected decent housing, healthcare and jobs, but instead they found the opposite.

One of the first things my nan remembers was how tiny and squashed together the houses were in England. Even if you were not rich in Jamaica, you had your own walls, but not here in the motherland, the 'land of milk and honey', or so it had been described. They had to help to build the NHS from the ground up, and they were often only allowed to take the lowest-paid jobs with the fewest benefits and least security possible.

I wonder whether Abraham felt a similar disappointment as he journeyed towards what he had been promised. Maybe he thought he would see the Promised Land in his lifetime. Did he expect the journey to be only five to ten years? Did he even imagine he would die and that not even his son or grandson would see it? After God's initial visit to Abraham in Genesis 12:1–3, when God invites him to leave everything he knows to go to a land he will be shown, their second interaction is in Genesis 13:14–17:

> The LORD said to Abram after Lot had parted from him, 'Look around from where you are, to the north and south, to the east and west. All the land that you see I will give to you and your offspring for ever. I will make your offspring like the dust of the earth, so that if anyone could count the dust, then your offspring could be counted. Go, walk through the length and breadth of the land, for I am giving it to you.'

At this point, Abraham is already past being a young man. His ancestors are recorded as living for way longer than we are used to today (his father Terah died at 205 years of age, according to Genesis 11:32). Abraham starts his great migration at 75 years old, so he may well be thinking that now would be a good time to start having these children if his descendants would really be as numerous as the dust. And yet, nothing. Sarah (called Sarai before her name change) is getting on in age. She is called 'barren' (Genesis 11:30, KJV). Their fertility challenges might to us seem predictable. We would not be surprised if a couple in their seventies struggled to conceive. But for them, who have received this promise from God, it is frustrating. It is hard to know how this couple could even know whether or not Sarah might be pregnant. Is she still menstruating? If not, are they just having sex and checking to see if her belly is growing? Despite the lack of signs that this could even happen, they believe it will. Abraham is spurred on when God tells him to walk the length and breadth of the land, since God will give it to him. But they are held in a tarrying moment, of waiting on God.

Abraham and Sarah are moving into the unknown, but they are in conversation with the God who leads them forward. The God who moved through the garden in the cool of the day, talking with the first people (Genesis 3:8), meets with, talks with and journeys with this family. God does not rule over them with force and fear, but gently guides, corrects and shows them the way. For some people, a God who dictates or rules with violence cannot be God at all. At least not a righteous, just or good God.

In light of Black people's history of survival and thriving against the odds, it is important for them to know God as one who recognises human agency. We are the descendants of those whose 'yes' has often never been sought, and whose 'no' has been ignored, including by those stating that they are acting in the name of God. The work of God in Black communities, families and individual lives is seen in the restoring of that ability to say 'yes' or 'no'. This is not to suggest we do not desire to know God's will or intention, but rather that we do not suppress our voice or allow others to take the place of God in our decision-making and discernment. Joe Aldred describes it as follows:

> I contend that the path to good decision making is when we combine the human and the divine, using the faculties God has given us even as we recognise our limitations in deference to the all-knowing God through prayer ... our human/divine relationship gives us faith that even though we don't know everything, that God who does will make up for our lack.[2]

The importance of including our thoughts, perspectives and rationale, alongside spiritual practices such as prayer, reinstates a sense of self that is much needed for Black people, especially Black women. Something similar could be said for women from all ethnic or racial groups who have often been taught to allow men in particular to decide for us, 'for our own good'. It may also resonate with those of us from working-class backgrounds, those living with disabilities and those from sexual or gender minorities who are denied the dignity of choice. Some of us have not always been and may still not be asked. Instead, others who do not know us as well as we know ourselves nevertheless presume they know best for us and can act on our behalf. To say that God exhibits these same tendencies is to make God nothing more than a bully, consistent with the 'pattern of this world' (Romans 12:2). We cannot be 'saved' by one who has the same habits as a violently racist manager who controls and threatens and dehumanises. We cannot be redeemed by one who denies the dignity of women or those living with disabilities. We cannot trust one who behaves as an exploitative employer. We must be saved *from* them.

The God who emerges in the experiences of Black believers is a God who calls to the ones who often go unnamed, unseen and unheard, and asks them to choose, to speak and to express their will. For this is God's will, that God's creation might flourish and thrive and be all it was intended to be. My grandfather's claiming of Abraham as a theological pin on which to hook his own experience is a reclaiming of his dignity and agency. In a world where men like him, from rural Jamaica and with a lack of formal education, do not get a say, he decided for himself as much as it was within his power. Full of faith and hope, he chose to make the journey, to say yes to the possibilities he might open up for his descendants.

As we sit with the story of Abraham, we find ourselves pondering many twists, turns and tensions. His journey of movement to finding a place to call home will resonate with many people, families and groups. How might this connection with Abraham affect how we think of migrants today? Have we ever considered the spiritual impact of people moving around the earth, including to the UK, or only the social, economic and political?

On the other hand, Abraham is a man with a sense of promise and purpose who proceeds to do harm to those who are vulnerable as he moves towards the future he hopes for. His wife Sarah is also involved in the abuse. In this, we are reminded that, even in our vulnerability, we can harm others. In our urgency and determination to do God's will, we are not free from the risk of failing to uphold the basic principles of loving those made in the image of God.

## Questions for reflection

1 In what ways do the stories of movement in your own life, or that of your family or those you are familiar with, resonate with the story of Abraham?

2 In what way do these patterns emerge in the contemporary life of the Church?

3 Who are the Hagars today – the people who end up as collateral damage in relation to Christian ministry and mission?

# Belonging

When I told my mother's mother that I was planning to apply for Jamaican citizenship, she laughed and replied, 'Fi wha'!' (why). Underneath her chuckle, she was intrigued. She and my grandad had done all they could to move to the UK, and here I was talking about claiming my citizenship to the island they had left. They had moved here in order to ensure a better quality of life for their children and descendants. They had experienced first-hand the limits that could occur on their beloved island.

My grandmother was academically gifted and loved school. Her brother was not interested at all and wanted to be a carpenter. Yet my great-grandparents, who wanted to ensure my great-uncle could provide for his future family, paid for him to continue his academic education. My grandma described this to me one day. She sat in her armchair, in her late eighties, explaining this story in the most matter-of-fact way. She was sent to train to be a seamstress, and she was amazing at it. I have seen many photographs of my mum and her seven sisters in dresses my nan had made. They were gorgeous, classy, custom-made and perfectly tailored. But she was sad to have missed out on an academic education.

Eventually, to her frustration, her brother dropped out of school to fulfil his own dream, but the money had been spent. She was not bitter or angry about this but was simply determined to live in a world where her daughters and granddaughters would never be overlooked as she had been. My mother's parents left Jamaica at the start of the 1960s, but returned in the 1980s. My grandfather had had enough of the weather, the racism and the struggle and decided to go home. They stayed there until he died. He is buried in a family plot, in the land of his birth but not the land of his ancestors.

To be Black and British is to belong to multiple places. I choose to interpret it this way, rather than to say I do not belong anywhere, though I know many feel this acutely. I belong in the UK, in

Birmingham, England, in particular, which holds all my memories of childhood and the history of my family. My family get-togethers are a rich combination of loud Brummie banter and Jamaican patois.

The first time I went to Jamaica, strangers on the road called me 'English *gyal*'. It was not hostile, but simply an observation. Maybe it was the way I was wilting in the mid-August forty-degree heat, or my Primark sunhat that gave it away. But I was excited to be in Jamaica with my whole family at sixteen years old. This was the island my grandparents had been born and raised on, and their culture, food, perspectives, language, humour and faith had been passed to my parents and then to me. I wanted to see the place where it had all begun. My parents were very relaxed, as was my grandad, but I could tell my nan was anxious. She knew we stood out and wondered whether we would be safe. Tourists in all places can be targets for crime, but she felt a particular wariness, maybe even shame, this this might happen to us in her homeland, in the place where we might have been born, had things been different.

I grew up in Handsworth in Birmingham, which was no walk in the park. I knew the tactics I thought would keep me safe. I was always polite to older people, giving them a smile and a polite nod of acknowledgement when I walked past, as I had seen my parents do. I knew to be vigilant as I walked past the predators hanging around in cars who tried to get my attention as I walked home from school in my uniform. I knew to be very careful in the winter, to not take short cuts and to stay on the same route I took every day. But Jamaica, I gathered from my nan, was a different kettle of fish. The levels of poverty coupled with the generational trauma brought on by the violence of enslavement and colonialism made it a volatile place. How do you create a good life going forward with so much unresolved pain in a nation's past? Families, communities and individuals live with trauma and carry it with them wherever they move to.

Going to Jamaica as an adult is an entirely different experience. I feel nothing but joy, as long as I can switch off my critical mind. On my last visit I sat with my sister on a beach in Negril, on the north-western coast of the island. As I relaxed with a cocktail in hand, the DJ doing his job exceedingly well, there was nothing that could disturb me. Not even the people with their sunhats on, walking down the beach selling everything from keyrings to coconut water to weed. The sun was warm on my skin, bringing out the brownest tones it could muster, and the cool breeze from the sea meant the temperature was just right. The sound of the waves lapping against the shore lulled my mind to rest and my soul to peace. The palm trees provided just the right amount of shade. And I was hit with two thoughts. First: God, you took your time when you created Jamaica. Second: how did my grandparents leave this? Not just why would they leave this place for grey concrete and rainy weather, but how did they muster the courage? It hit me, as I sat there, that this was all they had ever known. They had never visited England before they moved to live there. They heard stories about wealth, employment and opportunities and they decided to go. They prayed that God would help them to find homes and jobs, and to make a life. They walked into the unknown, armed with faith and determination.

Determination, faith and hope are the essence of Black faith, seen in that willingness to walk into the unknown. Black faith is courageous and stubborn in its willingness to persevere come what may, but also to say, 'Enough is enough,' when that moment comes. I arrive at this conclusion through the examples of my grandparents: my dad's parents who remained in the UK and my mum's parents who returned to Jamaica. I do not think either decision has more moral or theological weight than the other. They both teach us about Black life and agency, and about the ways of God who leads us sometimes in different directions.[3]

Processing this brings me again to Abraham and his descendants. We find a pattern as the story of Abraham's children continues, of siblings taking very different paths. Often these stories are shared in such a way that we find one party to have the moral high ground, but this is not always straightforward.

The conflict between Abraham's sons Isaac and Ishmael has nothing to do with them as individuals. The tension between these two brothers is down to the dynamics that surround their parents, the divine promise and the politics of inheritance. Their lives take distinct paths, and yet both in the end are blessed. In the case of Isaac's sons, we find again the problem of sibling rivalry, and the different paths brothers take. Jacob the *ginnal* (trickster) cons his brother Esau out of his birthright, leading to a breakdown in their relationship that spans years. In the end, the brothers are reconciled and both families are blessed despite initial periods of turmoil.

Probably even more famous are the twelve sons of Israel (whose name God changes from Jacob), the favouritism towards Joseph and his forced removal from his family. The rupture of an entire family is then undone years later when Joseph is reconciled with his father and brothers.

I am not suggesting there are neat endings to the patterns of migration, disconnect and disruption that so many families have experienced. And it seems that there are no easy answers to the questions of removal, migration and belonging. Remaining in the UK or returning home both involve struggle, compromise and challenges. There can be few places for some people to lay their heads. And yet God's blessing can find us wherever we roam.

The question of belonging can be complicated by many different factors. Race is one of the most obvious, but all aspects of our identity, including something as seemingly unimportant as an accent, can mark someone out as not belonging or not being the right sort of person for a particular group or place. Belonging can take determination, and sometimes we do not gain the benefits of the struggles we take on. I have the privilege of saying I belong in multiple places only because my grandparents and even my parents endured years of being made to feel that they did not belong. Each of us needs to be aware of how we might be contributing to the feeling of belonging or non-belonging for those around us, especially minority groups. This is the sign of a compassionate community.

## Questions for reflection

1 When you consider the places and spaces where you are now, to what extent do you feel you belong?

2 Where you have a strong sense of belonging, can you identify what and who makes that possible? How might you enable this for others?

3 Where you do not feel a sense of belonging, what tools enable you to cope? Are there opportunities for you to join together with others who may feel this way, even if it is for different reasons?

# Forced to move

Amid such a reflection on movement and migration, we cannot pretend that movement is always chosen. While my grandad identifies with the person of Abraham because he recognises his agency in leaving Jamaica, for many groups both historically and today, movement is not chosen at all, but is the result of violent forces beyond their control. In this sense, some communities might identify much more with the nations driven out by Abraham and Sarah's descendants.

The Canaanites are assumed to be heathens, godless and meaningless by those who claim to be acting in line with the will of God. Their lives do not matter; there is no dialogue, no conversation, only violence. They are forced to move from their land, when their land is stolen or their people are wiped out. This is enacted by those who claim God has commanded them to murder women, men and children. These passages in the Bible can be difficult to stomach – how do we reconcile this?

Part of the answer may lie in understanding that the biblical writers were influenced – as we all are – by the social and political context in which they wrote their accounts of history and God's voice within it. Biblical writers were influenced by contexts in which empires and their preference for violence and domination of others was normalised. Why wouldn't God also appear like this in their minds, if God is the greatest power of all?

The worlds in which the biblical writers developed the texts we now read were also contexts in which groups were assigned particular identities. As Fernando F. Segovia explains, fundamental tensions were seen between those people categorised as 'civilized/ uncivilised; advanced/primitive; cultured/barbarian; progressive/ backward; developed/undeveloped-underdeveloped'.[1] Violence was legitimised against those who were considered uncivilised, primitive, barbarian, backward or un/underdeveloped. This violence could very easily be spiritualised so that people would consider that it was God's will for such a group to be murdered en masse. The exploitation of people deemed 'backward', owing to their racial grouping, culture or class, is much easier when this is considered to be a natural or divine order. The stronger the narrative, the fewer the protesters. Abraham's descendants absorb these ways of seeing themselves as God's chosen and others as heathens worthy of death. God's name is associated with this violence, legitimising mass murder and genocide. The Church throughout history has done the same in countless times and places.

Forced removal has been a repeated aspect of Black community life that echoes into the present. The stories of the Windrush scandal are felt especially deeply by African Caribbeans because they repeat a history of forced removal. For our African ancestors – kidnapped, sold and transported across great seas – movement was not a choice. It is a difficult history to even imagine. An estimated 10 to 12 million Africans were forcibly taken from their homeland and enslaved to work for the wealth and development of Europe and America between the sixteenth and nineteenth centuries.

A mere century and a half later, the descendants of these Africans answered the call to come to the UK. They arrived not with plans of revenge but simply to exist and to create and to live, to rest and to remain. Few would have imagined that their status would be questioned years after the fact, that their movement would still not be over. Anthony Reddie describes this as the sign of being considered 'an enemy within' in Britain, which has particularly afflicted Black, Asian and Muslim communities.[2] Thousands of African Caribbeans, grown adults who had spent their whole lives here, including elderly African Caribbeans who had worked for decades in the UK, were again at risk of being moved against their will. Some lost jobs or were denied access to benefits to which they were entitled, while others were forcibly removed from their homes and families, detained and deported. More than twelve hundred individuals have come forward to claim compensation, while thousands more are believed to have been affected by a change in their status.

Movement has also become inevitable because of the impact of climate change, the trauma of history and the current decisions of the powerful in our world. Jamaica, like the wider Caribbean and many islands and countries around the world, is facing a bleak future in the coming years. The beach I enjoyed, pondering my ancestral stories and the beauty of creation, may not exist above ground in the years to come. The sea may rise and destroy the island it surrounds, when hurricanes, tornadoes or tsunamis strike. Black life, memory, movement and history are bound together with matters of environmental destruction and particularly the sea.

We know this, of course, because we are people of the land and the water. But if movement can involve the trauma of leaving one land for another, it often also involves a particular relationship to water. The sea, though often beautiful, can also be a traumatic place for Black people owing to our ancestral experiences of it. For generations of Black people, the sea represented forced movement from their homeland to plantations. Many of our African ancestors were thrown into the sea, whether dead or alive, from slave ships. Some threw themselves and their children from moving ships in order to spare them a lifetime of heavy labour, sexual exploitation and physical, psychological, emotional and spiritual abuse. The sea can be a traumatic place. The deep is not void at all.

Water, sea, rivers and channels have not ceased to be places of traumatised movement for communities today. While the transatlantic slave trade has ended, death in our global waterways has not. Few of us will forget the tragic image of three-year-old Alan Kurdi, a Syrian boy washed up on a Turkish beach after he and his family had fled Syria for Europe in 2015. The 'small boats crisis', which is really a crisis of hospitality, brings movement and the sea to the forefront again. The British government fails to protect asylum seekers, including children who are kidnapped by traffickers. Instead, our leaders make plans to hold refugees and asylum seekers on the *Bibby Stockholm* or to send them to Rwanda – unless they are from Ukraine. History repeats itself, as we deny people land and space to simply exist. And we seem to hope that the waters will cover a multitude of sins.

Forced movement, therefore, has the devastating effect of distorting our relationships with creation, with the land and with the sea. It turns beautiful aspects of the world into tools for evil and places of trauma. This is in addition to the harm that is done to individual people, families and communities. Understanding the interconnectedness of all things, as we saw in the last chapter, means we recognise that every action and inaction we take collectively has a wider effect. While we imagine we can abandon those we consider 'disposable' and remain unaffected, we in fact compromise our collective soul and negatively impact our human family and the goodness of creation.

## Questions for reflection

1 What do these historic and contemporary stories of forced movement tell us about the state of humanity?

2 Do these issues feature in your spiritual practice? How might including them help to overcome the dualisms that separate faith and spirituality from the urgent political matters of our time?

# Hostile environments

At the beginning of Genesis, we find a beautiful pattern of God's intention and desire for humanity, although we often follow our own designs of exploitation, domination and abuse. We make God in our own image. Abraham is called by God to move while tarrying. And yet his movements are not free from errors in judgement. Neither does movement bring him to what he hopes for. Abraham and Sarah receive the promise of a son, but they die without seeing the Promised Land, and so do their children's children. Their descendants journey in faith, based on a promise given not to them directly, but to their ancestors. In the course of their movement away from their homeland, the place of familiar abundance, Abraham and Sarah's descendants find places that initially feel safe.

Joseph, Abraham's great-grandson, arrives in Egypt against his will, but ends up being positioned to support his family and various nations at a time of economic crisis. Upon the reunion of Joseph with his brothers, he proceeds to invite his family to move to Egypt, a place of provision during a time of famine. God tells Jacob in a dream, 'Do not be afraid to go down to Egypt, for I will make you into a great nation there. I will go down to Egypt with you, and I will surely bring you back again' (Genesis 46:3–4). More movement. Jacob goes to Egypt for a joyous familiar reunion, after years of grief. He receives a joy he was not waiting for, but one that was awaiting him. When he dies, he is not buried in Egypt, nor in his ancestral lands, but with his ancestors Abraham and Sarah, in Canaan (Genesis 49:29–31). Joseph also, in his old age, asks that his bones be taken from Egypt when God leads them on to the Promised Land (Genesis 50:24–5). This would represent his final movement, even after his death.

In the years to come, Egypt, the place of provision, would become a place of oppression. The new pharaoh did not know about Joseph. How could this be possible? According to this biblical history, Joseph was prime minister, saved the nation from starvation and rescued the economy. How could this pharaoh not know? Was Joseph erased from the history books? Did they not want to attribute the progress of this nation to a foreigner? Joseph is written out of Egypt's history, and his people are now deemed a threat. The new pharaoh is anxious about the number of foreigners, and worried that they would not be loyal to Egypt in a time of conflict. He takes what he considers to be preventative action by enslaving them and removing their rights.

On the journey towards the promise, Abraham's descendants endure four hundred years of enslavement. They wait, generation after generation, for the deliverance of God. And while they tarry, they labour.

The people of Israel, when enslaved in Egypt, lose all hope for deliverance. When Moses arrives, they respond with cynicism and doubt, which is entirely understandable. Their ancestral stories are almost entirely forgotten. We do not find a record of anyone speaking about the God of Abraham, Isaac or Jacob and expecting deliverance. No one, like Joseph did, expects that they might move from this place and asks for their bones to be brought with them when they go. They are worn down by the lack of movement and generations of disappointment. The text tells us, 'The Israelites groaned in their slavery and cried out,' but it does not say to whom they cried (Exodus 2:23–4). Yet the writer does say that God heard and remembered them.

Tarrying in the midst of painful circumstances is, I think, one of the most challenging aspects of the life of faith. Whether tarrying is personal and private in your own life or related to the big trends of inequality, injustice and despair that shape our world, the in-between place can be agonising. We find ourselves in one place, facing one reality, while longing for another. When God is the one we hope will act on our behalf, the pain can be multiplied. Does God hear us or love us? Will God act, or are we on our own?

Tarrying in the midst of such moments depends on often very small movements that might even be undetected. At a particular moment of distress, we may find that God shifts the pain in our souls slightly by offering us a message of hope. In Black faith, this has often been how people have sustained their faith in unthinkable circumstances. Messages of hope have often been found and shared in songs, in scriptural passages and in personal testimonies. For Africans living under enslavement, the spiritual songs became a method for enabling them to endure mentally, spiritually and emotionally. They would speak of God delivering them – moving them on – from oppressive circumstances as God had done in the biblical text:

> Didn't my Lord deliver Daniel, then why not every man?
> He delivered Daniel from the lion's den
> Jonah from the belly of the whale
> And the Hebrew children from the fiery furnace
> Then why not every man?[1]

These songs served a dual purpose. They inspired the singers to remember God as a liberator and also enabled them to share coded messages among the enslaved population. When singing about 'heaven' or the 'Promised Land', enslaved Africans were often sharing plans to escape.[2] But escape was not always possible, and so finding ways to endure day by day and to keep one's God-given dignity alive in the process was essential. This meant that if or when the time and opportunity came, people were ready to move.

I believe we can learn something from these tactics, of active tarrying in the midst of trying circumstances. They speak to all people today who are seeking to endure oppressive circumstances, even when said conditions are maintained by people in the name of

God. Black people critically explored the theologies they received from their oppressors in the light of their lived experience and their reading of the Scriptures. These reinterpretations allowed Black people to recognise God as one who saw them and heard their cries, even when their 'Christian' masters did not. These methods teach us all how to keep our hearts fixed on God's words to us, which drown out the words and actions of those who undermine our humanity and right to exist. And they also tell us to be prepared to move when the moment of deliverance finally comes, in whatever manner it may arrive. This may not be a deliverance that comes ready-made in a particular heroic figure such as Moses, and Black civil rights history has proven that it is all too easy to cut off movements for liberation when they centre on individuals. Our deliverance may come as we organise together around shared interests, as we recognise our agency even while we tarry. It is sometimes through the small, underestimated acts, even a song, that we might begin to bring about the revolutionary change we tarry for.

## Questions for reflection

1 Do you identify with this story of intergenerational struggle and delayed hope? Are there echoes of struggle and hope in your own family?

2 What does the faith of those living in the most inhumane conditions teach us about the power of hope, and the ways God sustains and may deliver us?

# 4

# Spirit

In the previous chapter, we explored the theme of movement and migration in life and faith. This provides an avenue into thinking about the problem of human-induced climate change and the situation of so many groups in our contemporary world who are searching for a safe home and are denied it. I did not speak much about God as one who moves. But Steven Horne, who writes theology from within the context of Gypsy Roma Traveller communities, describes God in this way. In *Gypsies and Jesus*, he speaks about God as one who 'moves and adapts to the nature of His creation (hovering over the waters; hanging from a cross)'. This should not be read, in my view, as a suggestion that God changes in terms of God's core being, character and personhood. It is instead a description of the multiple ways God is seen to make Godself known to us as human beings in the Scriptures, and in our lives. In response, Horne explains that 'creation must move and adapt to the will of its God and Creator'.[1]

This suggests to me that we are invited by the moving God to move in response. As we discover new and greater expressions of God's ways with us, we are invited to broaden and deepen our thinking, our understanding and our faith. We are, in this sense, caught up in a dance with God, who teaches us the steps and then invites us to freestyle to the same rhythm.

In thinking of God as one who moves, we are led most easily to reflect on the person of the Holy Spirit. An often overlooked member of the Trinity – and I notice this especially owing to my roots – she is named as breath and wind in the Scriptures. Breath is the very basis for life and movement for our bodies and in the natural world. While not all movement, as we have seen, is inspired by God and invited freely, there are particular movements that, historically, Christians have recognised as direct moves by God the Holy Spirit. These movements have often arrived in the wake of much tarrying by the faithful in different places and times. It is to these moments of waiting and fulfilment that we now turn.

## The Spirit as gift

At the beginning of the book of Acts, the disciples are tarrying for the Holy Spirit. They are gathered in a room after Jesus has given them clear instructions to wait because he has left them a gift. Chapter 2 begins, 'When the day of Pentecost came,' but of course they did not know this was the day they had been waiting for when they woke up that morning. For weeks they may have been gathering together at every opportunity in anticipation of what Jesus had promised. Before work, after work, in their spare time, waiting together, praying and eating, even sleeping, in this place. They come back day after day, which may also mean they had been left feeling disappointed or disheartened on some days. How many days did they think, 'This will be the day when Jesus' promise is fulfilled,' or hope it would be, only to leave thinking, 'Was that it?' Did they fully understand what they were waiting for?

This tarrying for the Spirit captures the tarrying that so often shapes our lives of faith as human beings. We find ourselves waiting for so many things individually and collectively, not only as Christians but also as human beings. We wait for humanity to show greater love and compassion for one another, as we wait for the Church to reflect more of the life of Jesus. We wait for wars to cease and poverty to come to an end, even as we wait for the job we need, for our health to improve, for children, a spouse or a friendship to see brighter days. We wait for God to meet us, 'as the deer pants for streams of water' (Psalm 42:1). We wait for God together, to bring about the transformation of all that does harm to ourselves or others. We wait for God, hoping for the kind of power that might enable life, beauty, goodness and communion even in the midst of circumstances that so often oppose such things.

In the case of the disciples, we find that they are not disappointed: on one particular day, the promised Holy Spirit arrives, in a way that cannot be confused with anything else:

> Suddenly a sound like the blowing of a violent wind came from heaven and filled the whole house where they were sitting. They saw what seemed to be tongues of fire that separated and came to rest on each of them. All of them were filled with the Holy Spirit and began to speak in other tongues as the Spirit enabled them.
>
> (Acts 2:2–4)

For the disciples, there is no doubt here. None of the disciples is recorded as asking whether it is real, as Thomas did when Christ was raised from the dead (John 20:25). Maybe now that they have witnessed the resurrection, their doubts have been laid to rest. Or maybe, since it is happening within their own bodies, they feel even more connected to what is happening. Either way, the disciples feel sure about exactly what this moment represents, even though those outside the community of faith have doubts. The disciples are not simply guessing here; they are interpreting these occurrences through the testimonies and stories of their ancestors. They look back to those who have gone before them in order to understand what is happening in front of their eyes. Peter says boldly, 'This is what was spoken by the prophet Joel.' Explore.

The disciples are grounded in the midst of what feels like a new experience. They draw on what they have inherited and locate this new thing within the tradition they know. It is new, but it is also not new. They may not have seen this particular occurrence before, but they know that God has always been committed to being present among God's people. From the cloud in the day and the fire at night that guided them through the wilderness in Exodus, to the words and miraculous actions of the prophets and beyond – God has never been shy about ensuring God's people know God is present. Whether by taking on flesh to live and walk among them, or now by the tongues of fire and the gift of speaking in tongues, God is consistent in reminding God's people: you are not abandoned.

Christians across traditions and backgrounds today recognise this moment as that of the Spirit coming to the Church. But we also have different perspectives on what this moment represents for the Church today. For some, this moment is simply a one-off event, which means that the Church today is not only the body of Christ, but also the body in which the Holy Spirit dwells. All who belong to this body, because of this moment for the early Church, will share in this divine inheritance. Within this perspective, God has come to the Church as a whole through the Holy Spirit, and will abide in her and with her for eternity. There is no need for personal experience of this, since faith affirms that this is true. The Spirit will empower the Church to be Christ's witnesses in the whole world, in whatever place, time or context they are called.

For others, Pentecost represents a moment that Christians in every generation might hope for and seek after. Each individual might experience what it is for the Spirit to come to make her home within them. Each person might receive their own personal Pentecost, sometimes with the gift of speaking tongues as evidence that they have received this presence of God in their own lives. For such people, each Christian is empowered by the Spirit for living a holy life, sharing the gospel and exercising spiritual gifts and callings. They might then share in the miraculous life of the Acts 2 church in the contemporary world, especially through praying for healing and deliverance.

Of course, many will hold together elements of each of these emphases. However we understand it, it is a history-making moment for the disciples and the Church as a whole.

The arrival of the Holy Spirit is evidenced in the text by speaking in tongues. Debates continue as to the significance of speaking in tongues in this passage and for Christians today. In some contexts (often those that expect each person to have their own personal Pentecost), speaking in tongues is seen as the proof of one's Spirit baptism. This is what I grew up understanding in my Pentecostal church. Church services or prayer meetings often involved a commitment to tarrying for the gift of tongues. It was not enough to believe; one needed embodied proof that God had made their home within one's own body. Those who did not speak in tongues were encouraged to tarry some more.

Now, I have met some mean people who speak in tongues fluently. I have also met some of the most godly, loving and gentle people who have never uttered a word in a spiritual language. Speaking in tongues (like all spiritual gifts) without love is nothing; it is like a clanging symbol – making a scene with no substance (1 Corinthians 13:1). We must always avoid the trap of thinking that spiritual gifts or signs of spiritual power are evidence of a faithful Christian life. They can sometimes be nothing more than an illusion, designed to deceive. We have seen this exemplified in some of the stories that have emerged of spiritual abuse by charismatic leaders, believed to be gifted by the Spirit. The emphasis on celebrating spiritual gifts can mean that we do not pay attention to wider questions of a person's character and behaviour. The gifts of the Spirit should not be prioritised above the 'fruit of the Spirit', against which 'there is no law': 'love, joy, peace, forbearance, kindness, goodness, faithfulness, gentleness and self-control' (Galatians 5:22–3).

## Holy disruption

The Holy Spirit reminds us in this passage that God does not sit within the boxes we create. We can tend, I think, to have an idea of what comprises 'best practice' for God. We can look through the Scriptures and mentally underline the verses we like best, the stories we hope will play out in our lives and the characters we resonate with. We might want to be like Joseph when he leaves the prison and becomes prime minister, Esther who gets to save her people, or David who writes songs that go down in history. Maybe we focus on the Scriptures we take as personal promises, like the famous 'I know the plans I have for you' in Jeremiah 29:11. We can easily build our idea about who God is around these favourite parts of the Bible. God can easily become the eternal genie who must grant our heart's desires within our time frame, slay all our enemies and deliver us from everything we do not like. In the course of this God-construction project, we can tend to ignore the Holy Spirit altogether, or as much as we can.

God the Father or Jesus the Son tend to become our focus, and the Spirit slips from view. This may not be deliberate. She is more elusive. The Spirit may not always be comforting, despite her name. Jesus can be comforting to us because we see his actions and words very clearly. We can more easily quote him, interpret his actions and use him to support our particular argument – usually with other Christians. If we can arrive at so many different (and sometimes conflicting) visions of who Jesus is, as we interpret the eyewitness testimonies and oral histories we find, how much more complex is this when we attempt to say anything about the Spirit? The Holy Spirit is not so easy to categorise. She disrupts our pride. She humbles our attempts to have a handle on God, to presume we know and understand God. The Spirit undermines any illusion that we can hold God captive to our fantasies and agendas. She is like a wind blowing back and forth, such that we 'cannot tell where it comes from or where it is going' (John 3:8). Willie James Jennings explains it this way:

> The similitude of the wind to the Spirit's coming suggests not only its absolute power but its absolute controllability. No structure is stronger than the wind, and there is nothing beyond its touch. How much greater is the reality of the

Spirit than this weak metaphor? … This is God touching, taking hold of tongue and voice, mind, heart and body. This is a joining, unprecedented, unanticipated, unwanted, yet complete joining. Those gathered in prayer asked for power. They may have asked for the Holy Spirit to come, but they did not expect this. This is real grace, untamed grace.[2]

On the day of Pentecost, the Spirit arrives in a kind of holy chaos. It is holy because it is an act of God, but chaotic in relation to the order that as human beings we so often create, which are really kinds of disorder. It is so extreme that, although the disciples have a clear understanding of what they are experiencing, the people outside believe they are drunk in the morning. It is not neat or polite by any stretch of the imagination. Some hear the good news of God being declared in all kinds of languages. Others hear gibberish and write them off as drunkards. It is not a simple picture that onlookers can identify as a divine act of God. There are questions, doubts and uncertainty for those who do not know the prophetic words of Joel and cannot interpret what is happening through them.

I think that often, when we imagine an act of God, we expect it to be obvious to everyone. This is especially the case for those of us who inhabit or have inhabited the more charismatic part of the Church. We imagine that acts of God should be huge, and also obvious to everyone, especially unbelievers so that they might be converted. When such an act of God (at least in our judgement) occurs, we assume that everyone should immediately recognise it as something God has done. But in the story of Pentecost, we find that God's actions can be misunderstood and misinterpreted. For some, this is an act of God; others see human beings losing control and behaving in ways deemed inappropriate. Even those who love God do not always get it right.

This might seem scary to us, or counterintuitive. We can assume that we are responsible for making clear who God is and how God is with us. But this is not always possible, since God's thoughts and ways are not our thoughts and ways (see Isaiah 55:8). We might have an inclination, because we are speaking and living from within a history that continues to unfold and which began before we were here. We can draw on tradition and the insight of those who have gone before us to explain to others what we see. And we see Peter in particular taking his time to explain to those who might be unsure of what they are witnessing. But some things cannot be explained, and are not believed even when they are explained to the best of our ability. We are often living with unanswered questions in our own lives. We can be tempted to oversimplify complex moments, experiences or times in our lives and in the world, in order to provide an easy answer to ourselves or others. There is a kind of comfort that comes from this, but it rarely lasts. Our clichéd responses and well-polished answers are like a house built on the sand that washes away when the storms come. We might believe we should trust God, but it can be all too easy to trust in our own understanding and our ability to make things understandable.

When we face something we cannot understand or make understandable, we might respond in several ways. We might avoid the matter altogether, suppress our discomfort and choose silence. This is an easy option. It is a way to maintain a false sense of certainty and comfort that is rooted in denial. Second, we might try to make the complexity fit within a box we are comfortable with, even if that means we misinterpret what is happening. The onlookers are familiar with what it is to be drunk, so they assume that is what they are seeing, even though it is an incorrect assumption. Finally, we might pause our instinct to reject what does not fit immediately within our usual frames of reference and engage the spiritual practice of discernment, to see what God might be teaching us. This requires courage and faith; it is trusting that God knows all things and leads us to truth, even in those things we are just starting to discover.

This is an important way of approaching so many of the 'new' voices and perspectives that are being heard in our society at the moment. Our public conversations are full of ideas that many people have not heard before and are not familiar with. Our instinct can be to avoid or be silent, or to attempt to quieten those who make us uncomfortable. Or we caricature the unfamiliar, choosing to misinterpret each other because we refuse to listen in order to understand; we only listen in order to argue. Labels are thrown around, assumptions are made, and very rarely do we trust that the other is speaking from a place of genuine good intentions. We close down, when opening up is what is most needed.

The third option, that of open discernment, is where I believe the Holy Spirit meets us and allows us to grow in grace and truth. It is a space in which the one who does not understand, who perceives the situation as only chaos, might be led to find the holy. It is in this third space that a person with the patience of Peter might call us to attention and say, 'This is not what you think; this is actually a move of the Spirit of God.'

## Questions for reflection

1 How important is the person of the Holy Spirit in your faith and spiritual life? Is she overlooked, equally significant alongside the Father and Son, or the most acknowledged?

2 Do you have concerns, fears or negative experiences of charismatic gifts and spiritual practices? What underpins them, and what might address them in future?

3 How open are you to the unexpected and 'disruptive' in your faith? How do you respond to the 'holy chaos' of life, in which God challenges your perceptions and fixed ideas?

# The Spirit of justice

The day of Pentecost has an important place in the faith of many Christians, especially Pentecostals, who have named themselves after this moment. Black spirituality is not synonymous with Pentecostalism – though the latter is indebted to the former for many of its spiritual practices and theological emphases.

The spread of Pentecostalism is owing in significant part to a Black congregation and its minister at the Azusa Street Mission in Los Angeles. William J. Seymour is recognised as one of the forefathers of classical Pentecostalism, owing to his leadership of the mission, which was the epicentre of the Pentecostal revival that would sweep across huge parts of the world from 1906. In many pictures we have of this man he is wearing an eye patch, as he contracted smallpox and lost his left eye as a result. He was African American, handsome in a rugged kind of way, with a beard, and was relatively tall. He was born in Louisiana, in the South of the United States, and his parents were enslaved Africans. They were emancipated and he was born free to those unfamiliar with such a state of being. His people were traumatised by white supremacist violence and enslavement, and he would himself experience the evolving forms of racial violence in the aftermath of slavery.

Seymour was born to parents who were systematically kept in poverty and were forced to live in a segregated world with the crumbs from the table of others. But Seymour had an experience one day, as he attended a Holiness church in his home state. He knew in himself that God had called him, though he was an unlikely candidate. He was definitely not from the right class, or in the right skin, and he didn't have the right kind of education. But his calling had been verified by others in his community. Lucy Farrow, an African American church sister, even trusted him to lead her church while she was away working.

Seymour went to Bible college in Kansas in order to be trained for the ministry he had been called to. He was asked to sit in a segregated area outside the classroom by his teacher Charles Parham, a working-class white man who himself had known poverty. Within the churches these men came from, class was not necessarily a barrier to leadership, but racism continued to haunt these spaces which on the surface seemed multicultural. Nevertheless, the coming of the Spirit would disrupt the stubbornness of these realities, when revival came to Seymour's church on Azusa Street in 1906.

Los Angeles was a city where some Black people prospered in the early 1900s. A significant middle-class Black population existed there. African Americans ran businesses, owned property and worked in professional jobs. But these were generally not the kinds of Black people who went to the Azusa Street Mission, led by Seymour. Middle-class Black people were not keen on the shouting, dancing, speaking in tongues and general disorderliness common among the Pentecostals. The more well-to-do African Americans embraced aspects of their Black cultural identity that were familiar but would not make them look less sophisticated than their white middle-class counterparts.

Azusa Street was the site of radical, Spirit-led chaos. These believers did not care much what wealthy white people or anyone else thought. They were desperate to experience God as they read about in the book of Acts, and this was what they prayed for. They called it a 'revival', a moment of being energised, revitalised and empowered by God's Spirit. As they gathered to pray, they became overwhelmed by the sense of God's presence. Many responded by repenting of their sins and accepting Jesus as their Saviour. Those who had sicknesses reported being healed on the spot, and many spoke in languages they had never learned. People shouted for joy, rolled on the floor and danced together until they sweated. They cried, laughed and prayed until they lost their voices. They were working-class Black folks, washerwomen, labourers and those working in the service industry. In their daily lives they were low on the scale of importance, but here they danced in the presence of God's own self. This was what freedom felt like. In *The Apostolic Faith* newspaper, where accounts of the revival were recorded, one observer wrote:

> In a short time, God began to manifest His power and soon the building could not contain the people. Now the meetings continue all day and into the night and the fire is kindling all over the city and surrounding towns. Proud, well-dressed preachers come in to investigate. Soon their high looks are replaced with wonder, then conviction comes, and very often you will find them in a short time wallowing on the dirty floor, asking God to forgive them and make them as little children. It would be impossible to state how many have been converted, sanctified and filled with the Holy Ghost. They have been and are daily going out to all points of the compass to spread this wonderful gospel.[1]

But this was not the most stunning thing for those who attended and those who observed. The most unexpected outcome of this revival – the thing that those praying may not have even hoped for – was a turning of the tables towards welcome, equality and belonging for all people. Seymour was committed to this vision of a church in which all people could belong, even if this was not what his teacher Parham had had in mind. But it was not easy to accomplish. The wider political scene promoted white supremacy and segregation, and white Christians often followed suit. In many cases where churches were ethnically mixed, white people still held the power.

But at Azusa Street, this Black working-class congregation, led by the son of formerly enslaved Africans, prayed for revival, and the Spirit came. Some white people admitted that they did not even want to be there because of their racism, but nonetheless they felt drawn by the Spirit and could not stay away. The coming of the Spirit brought people together into communion across racial lines and disrupted the domination of white power that shaped wider society.

Latino and Latinas are also included in the early accounts of the revival, as are early travellers from India. They were drawn by the hope that they too might experience this Spirit-filled community that overturned racial categories. People arrived from across Asia, the Middle East and Europe to experience this spiritual revival in this relatively poor church building on a street on the 'wrong side' of town. While in the wider world the problems of class and race would undermine love and justice, in the revival, at least for a while, these norms were overturned.

Azusa Street is often heralded as the start of classical Pentecostalism, owing to its ripple effect around the world, but this was not the first time the Spirit had made her presence known in unexpected places. In 1905, a revival began at a mission for young widows and orphans in an area called Tinnevelly (now called Tirunelveli) in the Indian state of Tamil Nadu, South India. Pandita Ramabai was the leader of the mission where they began to pray for an experience of the Holy Spirit, and they received what they prayed for. Young women received this baptism in the Spirit, spoke in tongues and experienced other supernatural experiences.

In 1906, entirely separate from the Azusa Street revival, a similar occurrence took place in Pyongyang, South Korea. In this context, Koreans were living under Dutch colonialism, including in the Church. Koreans were not permitted to lead churches themselves, nor to develop their own theology or spiritual practices that were culturally relevant to them. When the revival broke out, it called into question the racist hierarchy that was evident in those spaces.

The Dutch church leaders began to ask: if the Spirit is filling Koreans and entrusting them with her gifts, then why are we withholding leadership from them?

The Welsh revival that took place at a similar time, in 1904–05, is a similar story, this time in relation to class. In this context, a working-class Yorkshireman, Evan Roberts, became the person named as the leader where this revival took place. Roberts left school at the age of eleven to work in the coalmines with his father, and he grew to be a preacher in the working-class communities he belonged to. When the revival came, his ministry would serve many people who travelled to Wales from around the world.

In the mid-twentieth century, a revival took place among Gypsy Roma Traveller communities in Europe. Though hated, treated with suspicion and violently persecuted, they experienced the presence of God in charismatic ways, first in France and then elsewhere, including the UK.

This important and often overlooked element of Church and charismatic history is consistent with so many stories we are more familiar with, including Azusa Street.[2] The Spirit is made known time and time again among the undervalued in the world.

I want to suggest that these occurrences should not be considered to be accidental. It matters, when those on the edges or at the bottom, in the order of the world, cry out desperately for God, that God is understood to answer. It should be an encouragement to us all, and a reminder that God does not share our common ideas about who is important or deserves to have their voice heard. In this sense, Pentecostalism is an important contributor to the body of believers around the world. As a movement from the outset among African-descended peoples, white communities, Asians and Latin Americans, it is truly a global faith. But it is also a spirituality that is located among those often overlooked in the world, because of race and/or class. It is a celebration of God's promise to lift up the lowly. As I have explained elsewhere:

> Pentecostalism is ... a movement of the Spirit that begins among 'the last'. While this may seem to be a purely spiritual occurrence, in actual fact, it signifies the birth of an alternative model of community that opposes existing political orders. In each of these contexts, the experience of Pentecost is outworked in challenging unjust structures even when they exist within the church itself. The work of the Spirit involves reordering the community of faith, in order to make of it a prophetic sign.[3]

Pentecostalism is recognised as one of the fastest-growing forms of Christianity around the world, for reasons that we do not have space to go into in great detail. But part of the reason is because it offers real hope and cultivates expectation among those often at risk of feeling hopeless or affected by despair. The emphasis on encounter with the Spirit is experienced as an empowering for individuals. And in many contexts, people experience an abundant spiritual life through their connection to God and the community of faith. This is despite what is happening in their own lives or in the wider world that might cause people to be discouraged.

Every person who is filled with the Spirit is taught that their life matters. This is especially important for those who live in bodies that may be presumed to be foreign, strange or queer; or inferior owing to race, gender, disability or simply not having the right status. Pentecost represents a moment of radical inclusion for the early Church. The coming of the Spirit means that people from all parts of the world are given a view into this movement of God among God's people. It throws the doors open for people of different cultures and from different places, and gives them room. The start of the Pentecostal movement, as a gift to the Church, expands this embrace and encourages us to follow suit.

## Questions for reflection

1 How might this idea of radical inclusion and reordering of unjust structures shape your understanding of the Holy Spirit's ministry in the Church and the world?

2 In your own context, are there people whom you or others consider to be less important or less likely for God to choose to be present among? What feeds those prejudices?

3 How do these stories of Pentecostal revivals reordering unjust dynamics broaden the ideas you may have of charismatic spirituality?

## Abiding with the Spirit

While I have been speaking about the work of God among the collective, there is also room to dwell on the ways of the Spirit with and within each one of us. This is never for the sake of personal ambition and selfishness. Nor does it mean the Spirit is with us in an isolated, individualistic manner. We are a body and a family. The Spirit of God in me joins with the Spirit in you confirming we are siblings in Christ, birthed by the same Holy Spirit.

My most recent experience of this was at an event I was asked to speak at on a Saturday evening. I hardly ever accept weekend invitations, but on this occasion when I saw the email and was about to reply with a polite decline, I felt the Spirit's nudge. The feeling grew that I needed to accept, and so I did. After preaching for their evening session, I stepped down from the stage and got ready to leave as the service was ending. I checked the train times, and the next one was at 22:18. I again felt a nudge and a feeling that I needed to hang back.

After a few seconds, a man came up to me with a headset on, he was an interpreter who had introduced himself earlier. He had come with a group of Roma women who were hoping to work with young people in their local communities. They were inviting me over to pray. I went over very happily, and looked forward to these women praying for me. I smiled, said hello and sat down with my eyes closed, waiting patiently. After a few moments I opened one eye and saw them waiting expectantly: I was the one who was being asked to pray. I nudged the interpreter and asked whether he could invite them outside, since the music was loud. One by one these ladies of varying ages got up, collected their handbags and followed us outside.

The first lady came up to me while the others hung back, and I knew they wanted me to pray with them as individuals. One of the staff members came over, looking concerned, and mouthed, 'Sorry, are you okay?' and I nodded. This was familiar territory for me. I grew up in a world where we prayed with each other as individuals, and tarried, just in case God wanted to use us to give a specific word of encouragement to the person. It had been a while since I had used these muscles, but I felt at peace.

I prayed for the first woman, who looked to be around my age, and she hugged me tightly and thanked me at the end. The second woman came to me, a matriarchal type. She was serious but kind, like so many of the women I had grown up around, and a similar age to my aunties. She told me what was happening in her family, asked me to pray for her, and I closed my eyes. I can only say that, as I tarried in the quiet before I prayed, I felt overwhelmed by love for this woman. No language barrier could have stopped the feeling I had that this woman and I were family; it was almost like I knew her. In that moment, as I waited for the Spirit, I felt a connection to her that cannot be explained. It was the same connection I have felt all my life as I have prayed and been prayed for by aunties, grandmothers and sisters in the faith. As the interpreter repeated my prayer for her, he began to cry.

My heart was so full, meeting these women and sensing their courage, which reminded me of my grandmothers, my aunts, my mother. They were not people many would choose to spend time with, because of gender, race and ideas about class. But they are those with whom and in whom God's Spirit is pleased to dwell. The Spirit bore witness not only that they were God's children, but also that we belonged to each other.

The Spirit of truth leads us to the truth about all things. The Spirit leads us to the truth about God, which then leads us to the truth about ourselves. Upon discovering the truth about God, whose love, righteousness and mercy abound, we can do nothing but respond with humble adoration. This worshipful heart is brought about by the spirit who leads us to cry out, '*Abba*, Father' (Galatians 4:6).

This humility is not a matter of self-hatred, of course, but a matter of thinking of oneself as one should. We often think humility is threatened only by pride. When we think too highly of ourselves, this is clearly a matter of the heart that must be addressed and resolved. It is an easier trap for some to fall into than others. With entire cultures, social, economic and political orders built around the notion that particular people should be listened to and treated with respect, is it no wonder pride can grab hold of so many. We think of such groups as privileged, and yet in spiritual terms they are deeply vulnerable. They live, teetering on the brink of all manner of sinfulness and evil, rooted in pride. They have believed the lie that they can and even should be like God. This can show itself in the tendencies we might have to judge who is worthy of love, mercy or kindness and who is not. Or maybe in the ways we use our power without collaboration or consultation to determine the state and purpose of other people's lives.

When we come to God in pride, in thinking of ourselves too much or too highly, and we come face to face with Jesus, he calls us to see ourselves as we are. As he spoke to the men who were eager to throw stones at the woman caught in scandal (John 8:1–11), Jesus asks us, 'Are you really righteous enough to approach this moment in this way?' Jesus' words are never intended to shame us, but simply to remind us that pretence is useless and unnecessary in God's presence. The facade by which we convince other people that we are 'good' and 'worthy' is unwarranted. God sees us more fully than we see ourselves and is never repulsed, disgusted or angered. As the Holy Spirit convicts me, I am suddenly aware that I do not need to have my guard up. I can lay down every strategy for defence, every argument, every agitation. I may recall something I have done, felt or thought that brings me shame, and rush to suppress it or defend it. But if I give the Spirit space, in the quiet, she will remind me that I am fully known and fully loved. She is my advocate, and Christ intercedes for me, and I need no self-defence.

True humility is undermined not only by pride, but also by low self-esteem, even a self-hatred. This kind of inner crisis puts us at risk too, since we still do not think of ourselves as we ought to. We can be easily afflicted by this condition, when socially and culturally we are convinced that we are not worthy of God's love or of the respect of others. We are taught – sometimes subconsciously, because of the people who are held up as examples – that we are valued less when we are older, or live with a disability, or are not considered attractive by the ever-evolving standards of beauty. We can be taught to second guess those from minority ethnic groups in the UK who are stereotyped negatively, women, those considered to be from lower classes, those who identify as LGBTQ+ or those with certain accents. Underneath all of this can be the sense that some were not included when God called humanity 'very good' in the beginning (Genesis 1:31). Somehow we are broken and in need of training, fixing, improving. When we internalise this, we give up our voice, lie about our desires and suppress our hopes because we are led to believe that we do not deserve to have them, let alone have them met.

In the presence of God who is 'I am' (clear about who God is), we are met with a gentle invitation to shift our gaze. The Spirit who knows God's mind (see 1 Corinthians 2:11) communes with our spirit who knows our mind. And God, whose life flows through us, abides with us and we with God. For God to abide with us means God is able to understand how we are wired, how we think and feel, and what we think and feel. It means God knows what we consistently need at our core, and also in a particular moment. It means that God is close enough for us to hear God whisper the words of life.

When we see ourselves as lower than God has made us, God's intention is never to leave us this way. In the moment when we are weighed down with the burden of false ideas about who we are, we are invited to lay it down. This opportunity to lay down our defences is revolutionary for those of us who are committed to pushing for a new world in one way or another. The fight for things to change in ourselves, in our family, community, country or the world can be taxing on the soul. In spiritual terms, we can experience a kind of warfare as we fight against the evils that so easily undermine life and flourishing for ourselves and others. But though warfare is necessary, we cannot live well in a state of constant high alert, especially one rooted in our feelings of unworthiness. Chichi Agorom puts it this way:

> There is a difference between fighting to *prove* we are worthy and fighting to create a new world *because* we know we are worthy of it. When our fight is grounded in a belief in our inherent worth and dignity, we don't have to carry the fight in us everywhere like armor. We are not here to just fight and suffer until we die. We get to choose rest, ease and joy for ourselves. We deserve that even while the world is a raging dumpster fire ... We deserve that because joy is our birthright. Rest is our birthright.[1]

I have started to say to friends that my ancestors' dream for me is not just about having certain jobs or opportunities, but also that I get to rest when I need to. This involves resting the body through sleep and relaxation as well as resting the mind through creative outlets or physical exercise. It includes finding ways to bring calm to our emotions, which can be overstimulated, and finding culturally restful spaces to be ourselves. Rest should also shape our spirituality, as we give up the striving that undermines our peace with God. Rest is not something that is available to all people even today, those whose rhythms of life have been determined entirely by others in view of their economic interests. Here, Agorom reminds Black people that rest is our birthright, even in a world where there is so much more to do. This is true for all of us. Abiding with the

Spirit is one way to ensure this rest each day for every one of us. Abiding with the Spirit occurs in the time we spend in prayer and in the posture of hearts that are continually turned to God as we go about our business.

Our abiding with the Spirit will always transform our movement in the world. Filled with the breath of God, how could it be that we would remain stuck, rigid and inflexible? Our Christian life is a life of flow. It is an experience of being carried in the movement of the Spirit, sometimes feeling as though our feet are lifting off the ground, in ways that make us a little (sometimes very) uncomfortable.

In pondering the work of the Spirit and in particular her holy disruption, it has become increasingly clear to me that being led by the Spirit might – and arguably should – lead us to the kinds of choices, actions or thoughts that may seem counterintuitive when considered through the lens of our own rationality. This should not be surprising, since the Holy Spirit is the Spirit of God who took on flesh to make Godself known, and preached a message of a kingdom that stands in stark contrast to the patterns of the wider world. In churches we can become very familiar with these ideas, and particularly with the parables of the kingdom, through which Jesus seeks to help his disciples understand what he is bringing about in the world as it is. He paints these pictures, fully realising that his followers will not have the grace to follow him, to share this gospel or to embody his commands without the gift of the Spirit. This is why Jesus gives them the Spirit, so that they might have the power to be his witnesses (Acts 1:8).

What is it that the disciples are called to witness to in the biblical story of Pentecost? Well, they are witnessing to what they have seen of God in flesh who was born of a young woman from the kind of town from which no one expected any good to come. That as he grew in faith in God, and in favour with people often considered unimportant, people noticed something was different about him. That as he became a man, he began to do whatever was in his power to heal those in need. That he spoke words of hope to the overlooked and helped those considered social outcasts to have a place where they might belong. That he encouraged those who were trying their best to keep going and to resist unhealthy patterns that would bring harm. That he wasn't afraid to challenge the religious types who tried to keep God in a box and looked down on everyone else. That even though the powerful tried to end his life, they were shamed because he came back from the dead and proved God to have the final say over all forms of violence, sin and death. The Spirit empowers the disciples (and us) to live in the light of this story.

In our contemporary moment, this leaves us with much food for thought. What does it mean for us to be full of the Spirit of God and to be led by the Spirit in the light of what we have seen so far? It means first and foremost that we might expect God to be present with us and working within us in our day-to-day lives, and throughout creation. We can often speak without thinking twice of God being with us, and yet some of our deepest pains come from the feeling that God is absent from our lives in some regard, or from the world as a whole.

Sometimes the feeling that God is inconsistent can be the most complex thing to get our heads around. We pray about something relatively small, like a difficult phone call or something as trivial as a parking space, and it all works out. Yet the major issues, like cancer in someone we love, or fertility issues, go on unresolved – who can understand such things?

Pentecost and Pentecostalism in particular remind us to continually expect God to be present, and even to intervene in our lives in some way or another. I know this can be difficult for some to believe, or even be considered a delusion by others. If we experience deep disappointment, loss and grief, we can lose all expectation that God exists, let alone is present and acts. But the gift of Pentecostal faith reminds us that God exists, that God's ears are not deaf and that God's arms are not too short to reach us (see Isaiah 59:1).

To say that God is working within us is to recognise that when we are caught up in the life of God's Spirit and open to her movements, we are embracing a journey of our own transformation. In the same way that tongue, mind and body are enveloped in the Spirit and compelled to move, so we, as we tarry, experience God's embrace. The softening of a heart and its harsh judgements, the opening of our eyes to those around us in compassion, our eagerness to see the best in others and to forgive as we are forgiven: these become signs of the work of God within us. So, too, the righteous anger at the injustice of the world, the determination to do right by those who are vulnerable and the willingness to lay down one's privilege. The Spirit invites us to live in response to the humanity of Jesus who is God and who showed us the path to eternal life.

To speak of God working throughout creation is to acknowledge that the work of the Spirit does not find its centre in us but in creation, in which we live as inhabitants. Before the Spirit of God was breathed into us, she hovered over the deep, and had intent and purpose before we existed. We are as much an expression of the creativity of God's surveying Spirit as the rivers, trees, birds and mammals we live among. The Spirit has been and is working in parts of creation that we have never seen, are unaware of and might never get to witness. The Spirit causes the glory of God to be seen in parts of God's created world that only God will ever know about.

We humans do not see it all, and we do not know it all. Our lives are as a flower in the field (Psalm 103:15–16). And so we are called, I think, by this fact, to see ourselves as creatures who exist in this world only as long as the breath of God sustains us. The Spirit's life does not revolve around us; rather, we are caught up in her gusts. The breath of God, which brings life to humanity, brings life to all things. We are bound up with the created world, dependent on the earth for our life, life that finds its source in the life of God. To be led by the Spirit is to be led by this awareness, as we interact with the earth, as we consider our impact on the created world and all creatures, human and non-human.

I have suggested in this chapter that our openness to the Spirit should go beyond a focus on individual empowerment and spiritual gifts, even though they remain an important part of Christian spirituality for many people. The Spirit is the one who forms us as we abide in God's presence, and God abides with us. She cultivates in us the fruits of 'love joy, peace, forbearance, kindness, goodness, faithfulness, gentleness and self-control' (Galatians 5:22–3). She forms just communities by destabilising hierarchies that dehumanise and exploit people and by bringing about holy community. The Spirit leads us to welcome the mysterious, the sudden, the spontaneous in our lives with God and in our lives together. This is especially true in relation to how we embrace those the Spirit draws to us from the corners and the margins of our world and Christian communities.

## Questions for reflection

1 How have you been taught to see the Holy Spirit's presence and work? What are the passages or personal experiences that have most shaped your understanding?

2 What might be missing in your beliefs regarding the Holy Spirit? Do you give enough attention to her ministry in relation to your personal spiritual formation, your relationships with others, your relationship with creation or the development of just and welcoming communities for all people?

3 What kinds of holy chaos do you think are needed in your context or in the world at large? How might you pray or otherwise participate in this holy work of God?

# 5

# Quiet

In the last chapter, we focused on the Spirit as one who is present, moving within and among God's people. The Spirit has been recognised as dwelling in unlikely, dark places and among groups who can often be considered to be somehow lacking. In such contexts, the Spirit moves people to dance, cry, laugh and speak, in human languages and in spiritual tongues. This is to some extent what many of us imagine to be 'Black spirituality', one that is geared towards expression, vibrancy and sound. And yet, as with all human life, quiet has an important place within Black life and spirituality. From the early days of the Church until now, quietness, whereby a person may attend to the inner life, has also been an important element of Black faith. It has allowed women and men, young and old, to remember who they are in the eyes of God, in a world that for so long has denied Black humanity. Contemplation allows Black communities to keep our eyes on the one who has made us and who sustains us in good times and in moments of trial. It is to this that we will now turn.

## Finding quiet

It was a Scottish Anglican priest and an Irish Catholic Sister who first taught me silent prayer. Angus had founded the Centre for Theology and Community (CTC) where I worked, to support churches that were community organising. He was imaginative and full of ideas, committed to our development as eager graduates, and bold. But he held power lightly, and was always willing to let ideas or people go if he discerned that the Spirit was moving in a different direction from what he had imagined.

Sister Jo (as I called her) was a kind and straight-talking woman with short white hair, glasses and a cheeky laugh. She would pack a group of us into her small car and drive (often at great pace) to retreat days. As a chaplain she deepened my understanding of the Christian life and my capacity to find God in the darkness, and for that I will be forever grateful.

I was working with Angus and Sister Jo in East London, having arrived fresh off the train from Birmingham with many of my belongings. At CTC, we were a group of Christians from across traditions working with churches who wanted to be involved in community organising. We would run training and workshops, preach on occasion, and help them understand how organising could be a way for them to live out their faith in integrated ways. Our focus was on loving our neighbours, honouring one another's stories and committing to rebuild communities in ways that were geared towards justice and peace.

After I had received a month of training, it was time to do the real thing, and I started the busy work of meeting local leaders and listening to their stories. I planned one-to-one conversations with people from different community groups, faith leaders, school staff and people from the local council. Our aim was to organise local power to address the prevalence of payday lenders who were targeting those already in need, with high-interest loans. It was busy work, and it could easily become all-consuming.

Community organising, like many of the most meaningful kinds of activity, can take so much energy and even leave a person exhausted. Meeting people turned out to be invigorating for me, but listening to the wide range of fears and concerns that people carried could have the opposite effect. In one day, I would meet with many different people. One person would be worried about getting an NHS appointment as they awaited a diagnosis. This would be followed by a meeting with a parent concerned about whether their son would arrive home from school that day alive and well or be stabbed on the way. Another would be with a woman working in domestic services who was being exploited by her boss but couldn't report it in case she lost her right to be in the UK. My task was to help local leaders decide on a shared goal and work towards it, despite their differences. It was incredible when it came together, but at times it felt as though it took everything I had.

As a team, we knew that we needed more than a great strategy for our community organising, and more than even a brilliant theology to explain what we did: we needed to pray. We wanted to be guided by God as we undertook training and delivered workshops. We needed a spiritual practice to underpin our actions. We did not want to 'gain the whole world' (even for the sake of justice) and 'forfeit [our] soul' (Matthew 16:26). For all of us who are eager to serve God and see goodness and justice in the world, it can be so easy to lose sight of God in the busyness. We risk being like those in Matthew 7:22, saying, 'Lord, Lord, did we not organise, campaign and plant lots of new churches for you?', only for the Lord to reply, 'You did not let me know you.' These are challenging words, but a reminder that our spiritual practice, our time for prayer and for communion with God, in whatever way that happens, is what gives us life. This is the place where we are reminded of who we are, what this is all for, and who holds all of what we see and experience in this life and beyond.

Silent prayer sounded like an oxymoron when I first heard of it. I grew up in a church that liked words, and lots of them. We believed that God knew what was in our hearts, but we also really liked loud, passionate praying. Prayers included emotion, demonstrating that one's whole self was involved in that moment of intercession. This suggested that we could feel the weight of what we were bringing to God: our needs, the needs of others, or our thanks and gratitude. Speaking in tongues was also an important part of prayer, and in some sense a kind of meditation or contemplation. Praying in tongues, understood to be a spiritual language, is a prayer that cannot be understood intellectually or even explained. It is prayer that is believed to be initiated by the Holy Spirit in the believer, which then goes directly to God. Rarely will the person praying know (in a rational sense) what they are praying, or be able to explain it to another person. The gift of interpretation must also be given by the Holy Spirit. But, to my understanding at the time, all praying involved words.

I had never imagined that silence in prayer was possible, or even spiritually acceptable. Surely we had to, 'by prayer and petition, with thanksgiving, present [our] requests to God' (Philippians 4:6)? And this, I had assumed, must be about words. But in the quietness of this small office, with a candle lit, we sat in silence. Angus would invite us to sit with our feet firmly on the ground and our hands resting softly on our lap. He would invite us to choose a simple prayer, such as, 'Lord, have mercy, I am a sinner,' and to bring our minds back to this prayer when it wandered. Sister Jo would remind us that we did not need to judge ourselves or be harsh if our minds were distracted, but simply to notice and bring them back to that prayer.

It was in silent prayer that I learnt the mystery of being known by God beyond what I was able to articulate with words. It was in this space that I became comfortable in allowing God to look at all of me and to gaze on me – yes, me – with delight. This was not because of a very eloquent prayer, in which I used my best words. Nor owing to the piety I offered, with my long intercessions in which I used all the right biblical language in the correct places. But simply because I was there, and I was open, in the place that God had been waiting for me, and would always be waiting for me.

## Laying words down

Our world and our relationships depend on words, and the idea of giving them up can present a major challenge. From our earliest years we are encouraged to learn to speak using words, or sign language to signify what many convey with words. We express our desires through words, and ask for what we hope for and need, even as children. We learn to say our name, to identify ourselves to others. As we get older, we use words to communicate who we are in terms of what our personalities are like and what we do.

Words enable us to build relationships. We decide who we want to be around in part because of what they say and how they sound. We use words to express our opinions as we talk with others, to share our experiences and to tell the truth as we see it. Through our words we can try to convince others of what we see and think, or defend ourselves from the ideas others share about who we are and what reality is like.

Words have huge power and impact on us and on others. It can be difficult and even scary to let them go. The great African American mystic Howard Thurman puts it this way:

> It is small wonder that man tends to worship the sound of his voice and to give it an authority greater than anything that remains when all words have been said … Silence is not trusted; it is subversive; it must be hidden. Fear of silence is the offering which we place upon the altar of words. This is in part due to the richness of the experience of speech.[1]

We may not think that we worship the sound of our own voice, but this can creep up on us. If we are a person with power (and most of us have some, even if it is not as much as others), it begins when we notice the impact of our words. This can make us either more careful about our words or eager to use them more. When we recognise that people change what they think based on what we say, we can get some thrill from this, or we can recognise the huge weight of responsibility that now involves. Sometimes it is a mixture of both.

This is something to be aware of at a time when it is easier than ever for people to speak and be heard by a huge audience. This is the case if we have access to the right technology, and especially if we look 'attractive'. The rise in podcasting is one such example of our collective urgency to speak. As a podcast host myself, this is something I wrestle with. On the one hand, podcasting provides an avenue for people to spread ideas that might serve other people and enhance our experience of life and the world. But sometimes, podcasts are simply a way for a person to promote themselves, sell a product or build a brand, with ideas that are controversial or even harmful. It is all too easy to become popular by using words to affirm the worst of human nature: greed, hatred and narcissism. Some words are better not said.

But even if we do not consider ourselves to have great influence, our conversations can reveal a lot about what we think of our own voice. In our conversations with others, we might assume everyone is missing out if we are not speaking. You may well know what it is like to be in a conversation with someone like this. They barely take a breath, leaving no avenue for you to respond or give your own perspective. They do not allow you to finish your sentences but rush to cut you off or to recentre the conversation around their own words. You may have taken on these habits yourself. These are the subtle ways in which we might reveal that we do, even slightly, worship the sound of our own voice.

These habits can affect us when it comes to prayer. Entering into prayer, we can often prioritise what we have to say and our need to urgently express our feelings. We might rush to bring up all the issues that affect us, the incidents that have caused us pain or discomfort, and urge God to address them. We might bring many tears to çoat our words, as our hearts are in turmoil. This is understandable, and human. I do not believe God is annoyed by this. But I also believe that silent prayer, or contemplation, when practised, enables us to resist the domination of words that so often marks our speech in prayer and in life. Contemplation, as we continue to practise it, enables us to calm the mind as we still the tongue. We find ways to observe and to hold the thoughts and feelings that threaten to overwhelm us.

A passage that might help us to consider the importance of silent prayer is Psalm 131. I love the Psalms because I so often feel comforted by the fact that so many of them reflect the agitated, anxious prayer life that so many of us are familiar with. We find the full range of emotions, from joy and celebration to fear and uncertainty, confusion, disappointment and even despair. The psalmists do not put on a brave face in their prayers and songs. Psalm 131 is named as a Psalm of David and a Song of Ascents. In the midst of his busy life, with all of its pressures, the psalmist manages to calm himself and quieten himself. In the presence of God, he becomes content, like a weaned child with its mother. He says:

> My heart is not proud, LORD,
>     my eyes are not haughty;
> I do not concern myself with great matters
>     or things too wonderful for me.
> But I have calmed and quietened myself,
>     I am like a weaned child with its mother;
>     like a weaned child I am content.
> Israel, put your hope in the LORD
>     both now and forevermore.

David is not crying, grasping and desperate in this prayer, but rather he is able to simply rest in the place of abundant love and let go of the urgency of his needs and wants. How often do we find ourselves in prayer, with subtle pride in our hearts and haughty eyes? How frequently is our mind swirling with 'great matters' that we hope to bring to God's attention? Often we can speak a lot in prayer, as we attempt to capture things 'too wonderful' or too complicated for us. This is a constant battle for me. Yet somehow, with all of the great concerns and questions that must surely be on the mind of this shepherd boy who has become king, David is able to quieten himself.

I wonder whether this humility was developed in David through what he lived. Not only him becoming king, although he was raised as a shepherd boy in a rural community. But also by the way he was humbled by the message from the prophet Nathan after he abused his power by having sex with Bathsheba (who likely could not deny him) and then murdered her husband Uriah (2 Samuel 11–12). At a certain point, his heart was proud, thinking that because he was king and anointed by God he could do whatever he liked. But here, in this psalm, he seems to have come to a place of humility, seeing himself as he ought.

As with the weaned child sitting with its mother, so stillness often accompanies quiet. In our spiritual practice, a still body and tongue can sometimes enable a still mind and give room for spiritual communion with God. As we focus on the movement of our breath, a gift from God, we are reminded that we are living by the simplicity of our inhale and exhale. In this we remember that we live by God's grace and mercy alone. We shed the forms of idolatry that tempt us, as we realise that these created things cannot be the source of life. As we sit still and attend to quiet, we might even have the opportunity to reflect on the urgency of our daily movements. In resisting the urge to move and be busy, we exercise restraint, a spiritual discipline. We refuse to be conformed to patterns that demand we produce as much as we can. We deny the idolatry of busyness, growth at any cost and extraction. We declare with our bodies that we are more than objects, workers and producers. We are human, created by God, and for God first and foremost and forever.

## Questions for reflection

1 Do you benefit from silent, contemplative prayer in your own regular practice? If so, how does it enhance your personal rhythms? If not, what prevents you?

2 As you reflect on your own relationship with words, in what ways are you at risk of worshipping the sound of your own voice?

# Embracing quiet

The idea of quiet can seem counterintuitive when we consider the state of the world. How can we consider not speaking when there is so much to be said and done? It is difficult not to be overwhelmed by the many overlapping crises we are facing as humanity: the destruction of the natural world; the ongoing realities of racism, gender inequity and socio-economic disparities; the crisis of poverty, trauma and youth violence in our cities; sexual exploitation and abuse of children as well as adults. The list is endless. In addition, there are all the needs we are aware of in our own lives and in the lives of those we know and love.

Black spiritual perspectives have much to teach us about bringing everything to God. By promoting an integrated spirituality that encompasses all aspects of our lives, Black perspectives invite all people to ask, 'What troubles me, and how might my spiritual practices enable me to bring these things before God?' Rather than imagining that there are certain topics or themes that are spiritual, which I can bring to God in prayer, and others that are not, I am invited to bring it all. According to Black faith, God is interested in hearing about the boss who may be bullying you at work, the fears you have for your children, the concern for your loved one's mental health and the anxiety you have about the bills that need to be paid. God is also concerned about the oppressive political leaders who abuse their power, or pastors who misrepresent the gospel and hurt those in their care.

But through the practice of contemplation, we are able to see even these urgent matters with a better perspective. Rather than seeing only what is sinful and evil and being tempted to give in to despair, our eyes are lifted up to the one from whom our help comes (see Psalm 121:1–2). Contemplating God, as we embrace quiet, allows us to meditate on the beauty of God so that all else is seen in the light of God's presence and love. While focusing all of our energy on what is wrong in the world and in our lives might feel pragmatic, so that we can seek to change it, such a focus can so often lead to burdens too heavy for us to bear. Contemplation, in which we commit our minds to considering God's person and ways, is water for our souls that are so often dried out by the harsh conditions in which we live.

Abba Moses was an Ethiopian desert father who lived around 330–405 CE. He was also known as Moses the Black, and he wrote about contemplation as the practice of knowing God, which can take place in many ways:

> We know him in worshipping his very being which we cannot fathom, the vision, which is yet hidden, though it is promised, and for which we may hope. We know him in the majesty of his creation, in regarding his justice, in apprehending the help we receive for our daily lives. We contemplate him when we see what he has wrought with his saints in every generation: when we feel awe at the mighty power which rules creation, the unmeasurable knowledge of his eye which sees into the secrets of every heart; when we remember that he has counted the grains of sand upon the shore and the waves upon the sea and the raindrops, that he sees every day and hour through all the centuries past and future: when we remember his mercy unimaginable – seeing countless sins committed every moment and yet bearing them with inexhaustible long-suffering; when we contemplate that he has called us by reason of no merit which he found in us but simply of his free grace.[1]

Abba Moses invites us to let our minds wander on God, while recognising that we can never fully comprehend who God is in God's fullness. There are mysteries that, even as we think on them, we will never understand, and this is the joy of our human lives: we do not have to have all the answers or understand every detail.

Allowing our minds to contemplate God is a way to worship God with all of ourselves, with our minds and our imaginations. It is a way to release ourselves from the heaviness of our current life and to gain a perspective that allows us to inhabit our reality with grace and peace.

Abba Moses encourages us to be open to the myriad ways and contexts in which God might meet us. Creation often points so many of us towards God the creator. Being in the natural world is one way in which people, whether or not they consider themselves to be religious, feel connected to others, to the divine or to a 'higher power'. The beauty of beholding what we have no power to create or control can lead us all to contemplate the big questions about our existence. They are things for which we might be grateful, and we may even be moved to worship.

Words are not the only option for those who are deeply concerned with the state of the world. Choosing quiet can be a very powerful practice for those hoping to reclaim their humanity beyond what they suffer and have survived. In *The Sovereignty of Quiet*, Kevin Quashie explains how important it is that we do not see everything Black people do through the lens of racial oppression and resistance. This is always a risk when we name what people have endured that we end up seeing them as victims. If someone survives trauma or abuse, we call them 'a survivor', which is better than 'a victim' but can still tie a person's whole identity to what has been done to them by someone else or some other group. This is something we must guard against – we are more than what has been done to us. Quashie goes so far as to argue that when we imagine Black people as a whole to be categorised by struggle, protest and survival, without recognising the importance of quiet, this is a kind of racism. Sometimes it is internalised, meaning that as Black people we begin to believe that quiet is not for us to enjoy. Quashie explains that even in moments we might think of as resistant and political, we must always recognise the quiet:

> Quiet ... is a metaphor for the full range of one's inner life – one's desires, ambitions, hungers, vulnerabilities, fears. The inner life is not apolitical or without social value, but neither is it determined entirely by publicness. In fact, the interior – dynamic and ravishing – is a stay against the dominance of the social world; it has its own sovereignty. It is hard to see, even harder to describe, but no less potent in its ineffability. Quiet. In humanity, quiet is inevitable, essential. It is a simple, beautiful part of what it means to be alive. It is already there, if one is looking to understand it.[2]

Quashie is making the point that Black people live, have joy, love, speak, write poetry, laugh and create art for their own sake, not always in response to racism or to resist injustice. In other words, Black expression is not always *saying* something; sometimes it just *is*. This is a very important point that humanises Black people, as we, like all people, need space to simply *be* without having to fight.

Of course, we all benefit from the many people who have fought, written and spoken against harm and evil. Some of the most important moments in the fight for human dignity, life and thriving have revolved around words. But Black people and all those who might struggle in the world should also have permission to be quiet, to contemplate beauty and to create what gives them and others joy. This is core to what it is to be human. Everything does not need to be a protest. We do not exist to prove wrong those who despise or doubt us. If, as writer Toni Morrison famously stated, 'the function of racism is distraction',[3] then how might we be less distracted? The answer, I am sure, will involve some quiet.

Being human means that we must keep on paying attention to what is happening within us, rather than focusing entirely on what is occurring in our social and political context. If we fail to do this, we risk becoming exactly what we are fighting against. Quiet gives us the space to allow God to do God's work within us, to free our hearts from what is destructive and opposed to love and to open them to all that is good.

## Questions for reflection

1 Do you struggle to see the value of quiet in a world in which there are many urgent needs and issues to speak about and act on? Or is quiet a gift to you because of this?

2 Is there a space where you find it easier to contemplate God? What leads your mind to wander on the subject of God's goodness and presence in the world?

3 Do you give space to attending to your inner life, or are you more likely to neglect it in the busyness of work, ministry or social relationships? What, if anything, might need to be addressed here?

## Finding God and ourselves

Silent prayer can be transformative, through its capacity to overturn harmful forms of silence or silencing. In our discussion of quiet, we must also remember that there are some groups who have been forced to be silent. For some people, letting go of words is not a choice that they have. In some cases, words are stolen or suppressed. Silence has shaped the lives of women who have not been allowed to vote, or have been rendered voiceless in families or churches. Those from the working classes have had to fight to be heard as their voices and interests have often not been recognised by those making decisions. Those of us whose ancestors experienced colonisation live with the consequences of being forced to give up languages or political voice. Children have often been expected to be 'seen and not heard'.

Some of the most horrifying accounts of the silencing of children have been brought to light in recent times, in the stories of child abuse in churches across traditions. Abusers have sought to prevent survivors from using the power of their words to speak about what has occurred. Even when survivors have the strength to speak, sometimes as adults, too often they are not believed.

It is important to realise that enforced silence undermines a person's life in a holistic way, including the life of prayer. Quiet or silence has to be chosen for it to have the possibility of playing a positive role in our spiritual formation. Healthy, spiritually nurturing silence occurs when we choose not to speak, from a position of knowing that our words have value and our voice is welcomed. For survivors of all kinds of abuse or violence, silence may be part of our spiritual journey at some point, but most immediately, what might be necessary is that we are free to articulate to God and others exactly what has happened, in as many words as we need. Enforcing silence is tantamount to a form of secondary abuse. Choosing silence, on the other hand, can open up the space for us to still the trauma and pain that threatens to overwhelm us. It can be a space to notice and process emotions and to be met by God in that. Finding friends and supporters to accompany us in that process is often crucial.

Sarah Coakley writes helpfully of contemplation in response to the problems of power and submission that affect us all. Thinking specifically about women – although I would say this relates to all who experience forms of powerlessness in society and the Church – Coakley invites us to embrace contemplation as a means of holding our own power in ways that reflect Christ. Some have argued that we must reject the idea of submission altogether, owing to the risk of further oppressing those already pushed into a lower position. But Coakley suggests it is an important part of our Christian life before God that we can reimagine so that contemplation functions as a space for empowerment as we make space for God:

> We can only be properly 'empowered' here if we cease to set the agenda, if we 'make space' for God to be God ... engaging in any such regular and repeated 'waiting on the divine' will involve great personal commitment and (apparently) great personal risk; to put it in psychological terms, the dangers of a too-sudden uprush of material from the unconscious, too immediate a contact of the thus disarmed self with God, are not inconsiderable ... But whilst risky, this practice is profoundly transformative ... it is a feature of the special 'self-effacement' of this gentle space-making ... that it marks one's willed engagement in the pattern of cross and resurrection ... 'Have this mind in you', wrote Paul, 'which was also in Christ Jesus.'[1]

Reading this, we find a description of the complexity we experience in the place of contemplation, which we often avoid. In the first instance, we find the vulnerability of 'not setting the agenda' when we so often arrive at the place of prayer weighed down with heavy concerns. Practising contemplation – as a practice we grow in, not a skill we fully acquire – is the practice of generosity towards God. In making space for God, we reciprocate what God has done by first making space for us within God's own life.

Contemplation can feel something like inviting a person back to your home for dinner. The day before, you might plan the meal and ensure you have all the necessary food items. You might even prepare anything that needs to be done in advance, especially if something needs to be marinated overnight. The next day, you may spend time making sure your home is clean, especially the rooms where your guest will sit or eat. You make sure there are fresh towels in the bathroom and you let some fresh air in as you vacuum and dust. You hope to make a good impression. And then the guest rings the doorbell, you open the door and they walk right in. You offer them a seat and a drink, and then their eyes start to glance around, and they ask whether they can have a tour of your home. You say, 'Sure,' but are nervous because in truth you shoved all the bits and bobs in one of the rooms and pulled the door shut. And you didn't expect them to go upstairs, and it is a total mess. So you show them the nice rooms, but they are not satisfied. They want to see it all.

As with a guest invited into our home, we cannot be quite sure exactly what God might say and do, and herein lies the apparent risk. What might God say as God makes God's home in our lives? Will God have opinions and thoughts on what we have and the state of things? We might immediately be filled with concerns and the fear of shame. We might even begin to regret offering the invitation. This fear of God's gaze might reflect the fear we have of our own thoughts, and what might be unearthed as we sit with God in the stillness. What hidden desires and thoughts are we suppressing with our busyness? What fears and doubts do we stem with noise? These are rushing towards us in the quiet; this is the 'too sudden uprush of material from the unconscious'. The risk is real, and yet we are invited to take part regardless, for the reward is significantly greater.

Coakley speaks about 'self-effacement', and it is important to consider how this can be understood in ways that are healthy and spiritually enriching. This is especially important when so many of us can, for different reasons, be given the impression that we have to erase parts of ourselves in order to be accepted by others, by the church or by God. Carlton Turner calls this 'self-negation' when he discusses what can happen within African Caribbeans, particularly Bahamians. While Bahamians have a rich culture, combining many traditions and elements, especially those from Africa, many Christians are made to believe that they have to reject them because they are not European. He explains: 'Indigenous, mainly African cultural modes of expression, languages, art forms, and even African Religiocultural retentions like Junkanoo (carnival), are seen by Caribbean Christians themselves as improper and second class at best and evil or demonic at worst.'[2]

This is one of the effects of colonialism in this region, but this kind of self-negation can occur for a whole range of people. It is relevant for those of us whose history has been disrupted by colonialism and the slave trade, but similar patterns can emerge for others who are required to lose parts of themselves to fit into the world or the Church. In contexts that value the white, middle-/ upper-class, heterosexual, able-bodied man as the best form of what it is to be human, all those who do not fit this are, at some level, required to practise forms of self-negation to belong. If not, you risk being sidelined, considered a troublemaker or just 'not the right fit'.

But this is not what Coakley is encouraging us towards, in my view. The differences between an unhealthy 'self-negation' and what is described positively as 'self-effacement' are in the motivation and the impact on the person's inner life. Self-negation is motivated by fear, by the belief (often given to us by others) that we cannot be ourselves if we want to be accepted by others or by God. Self-negation is what occurs when we anticipate rejection and have been made to doubt our worthiness of love, or our status as image bearers of God.

This can begin in our relationship with others and filter through to our perceptions of God. Or it can begin with the theologies we have inherited, which tell us first and foremost that we are broken, sinful and evil before we are good. Self-negation is hatred of the self, and it can lead to the hatred of our neighbour. Since we cannot be free, we refuse freedom to others. It stands in the way of gentleness and kindness with our neighbours, since we have only ever learnt to be harsh and unkind to ourselves. It denies the truth and prevents genuine love. Self-negation is a performance requiring the right lines, the costume and the necessary make-up. It is a spectacle designed to make us acceptable. We perform it for others and for God, and sometimes we imagine we have fooled everyone. But inside, our hearts are in turmoil, as our true life is suppressed. We exist out of sync with the God who made us.

Self-effacement, on the other hand, is motivated by a desire to know God and to be truly known by God. As we tarry before God, so the Spirit may blow over and through us, and we discover the things that we might let go of. We identify the heavy burdens we have held on to, thinking they make us who we are, when really they have only left us with bent backs and exhaustion. We allow God to say, 'This is something you might release, dear one.' We might need to let go of our desire to please others, which prevents us from honouring God's voice in our lives and how God has made and called us. We might need to release old desires, expectations or goals we have had for ourselves, as we evolve and change. We might learn, in the stillness, that even our hopes and desires can become weighty stones around our necks, anchoring us in places that are like deserts – dry and desperate. We might need to let go of habits or patterns of behaviour that are harmful to us or others. We might need to release the anger, the ill will or the hatred we have towards a person or people who have done us harm.

The systems we look to for justice may or may not be adequate, and we may or may not get the closure we need. But in the place of contemplation, we come face to face with one who knows what it is to be betrayed and is familiar with what we suffer. Jesus does not downplay what we feel or pretend it doesn't matter. But he can help us see when our hearts are being weighed down with heavy burdens, and he can invite us to lay them down.

In contemplation, we are met with the gracious kindness of God who never turns away in disgust or embarrassment. Instead, God holds our gaze, with deep love and radiating acceptance. In self-effacement, we give ourselves to God and God gives us back ourselves, full of grace and truth. The impact of this self-effacement is expansion, not erasure; depth and newness of life, not lack and deprivation. As we place ourselves in the hands of God, we trust God to sift it all and to give us back the treasures that are of eternal value.

## Questions for reflection

1 Are there contexts in which you are silent or silenced by others? What might it take for you to find your voice?
2 To what extent do you see Black people or other groups as characterised by noise and protest? What might it mean to defend the need for such groups to also have space to be quiet?
3 Do you resonate with the ideas of self-negation and self-effacement? How do they play out in your own spiritual practice or life in general?

# Contemplating God

In reflecting on contemplation, we must of course learn from those who have been most committed to it. Contemplation, the practice of silencing oneself in meditation and prayer before God, does not come naturally to people at any time. But I do believe it is a particular challenge for us today when we live in such a noisy world. We are bombarded all day by ideas, images and thoughts. Our minds are overstimulated, our brains are overwhelmed with advertising, entertainment and media, all demanding a response.

The desert fathers and mothers, as we call them, were people who fled their own noisy contexts in order to give themselves wholeheartedly to the contemplation of God. They committed their lives to the task of prayer and deep reflection on the mysteries of God. In order to make space for such a vocation, they would give away all their material possessions and any other financial commitments they would need to work for to sustain. And they would commit to a life of simplicity, sometimes in isolation, as hermits.

One such hermit was called Abba Moses the Black, mentioned earlier. I came across him when reading a book called *Every Tribe: Stories of diverse saints serving a diverse world*, edited by Sharon Prentis.[1] In it, Calvert Prentis writes a chapter on Abba Moses' complex past, his radical conversion and the contribution of his spiritual writings. Abba Moses began life as a slave in an Egyptian household before being kicked out and joining a gang to survive. While on the run owing to his criminal activity, he came across a group of hermits and was so affected by their lives that he asked to join them. However, as Prentis explains:

> The hermits were not convinced that such a hardened criminal could renounce a life of crime to pursue one of holiness. Despite their obvious reluctance to accept him, Moses

persisted with his request to join the hermits. Eventually, after testing him to see if he would revert to his former ways, they became convinced of his change of heart and fervent desire to follow Christ. He too became a hermit, spending long periods alone in prayer, living in austerity and devoting himself to serving the older monks in the community.[2]

Abba Moses, an unlikely desert father, would learn contemplation in this community of holy men who sought to give their lives entirely to contemplating God. In light of his own transformation, Abba Moses' reflections often focus on the importance of purity of heart. This is not a legalistic purity by which a person attempts to earn God's favour, but is rather in terms of the work of the Holy Spirit who forms holiness within us. In explaining the importance of contemplation as a spiritual practice, Abba Moses uses the story of Mary and Martha, recorded in Luke 10:38–42:

> As Jesus and his disciples were on their way, he came to a village where a woman named Martha opened her home to him. She had a sister called Mary, who sat at the Lord's feet listening to what he said. But Martha was distracted by all the preparations that had to be made. She came to him and asked, 'Lord, don't you care that my sister has left me to do the work by myself? Tell her to help me!'
>
> 'Martha, Martha,' the Lord answered, 'you are worried and upset about many things, but few things are needed – or indeed only one. Mary has chosen what is better, and it will not be taken away from her.'

I have always found this both a beautiful and a difficult story, as someone who has internalised the idea that it is good for women to be busy. You only need to look at church life to see this. Without women, the majority of churches would cease to function.

Regardless of tradition, ethnicity or culture, class or geography, women are predominantly the ones who attend churches and keep them going. I imagine, if we could be transported to churches around the world on any given Sunday, that we would see women of every shade, language, age and size being busy. Women would be seen cleaning church buildings, printing service sheets, arranging flowers, welcoming people, organising food parcels, making sure the chalices are clean and where they should be, preaching (if allowed), leading intercessions, serving communion, ironing the altar cloths, serving the tea and biscuits or patties at the end, and tidying up. But in this passage, it seems that Jesus is saying that, actually, that is not the best thing. Abba Moses draws our attention to Jesus' judgement that Mary has 'chosen what is better' and that this 'will not be taken away from her':

> So long as injustice prevails in the world, works of mercy are needed and will be useful to the man who practises them, and his godliness and good intention will make him an heir of eternal life. But in the world to come, when all men are equal, these works will not be needed. There everyone will pass from the multiplicity of different good works to the love of God and the contemplation of the things of God in an unceasing purity of heart.[3]

Abba Moses invites us to keep in mind the transitory nature of what we do in this life. And to ensure that those activities that can be taken away do not take the place of those things that will never be lost. If eternity will be a ceaseless contemplation of God and gazing upon God's beauty, then we are invited to begin to live this way even now. We must take time to gaze.

This can be a challenge when our eyes see so many things, even those things we know God is concerned about. In our eagerness to see justice and peace, we can spend so much of our time gazing at what is evil, sinful and messy in our church and in the world. And it is important that we see them. Abba Moses does not invite us into a kind of spiritual practice that denies the importance of seeing and responding. He does not condemn Martha, and neither does Jesus. Abba Moses recognises that our actions in an unjust world are essential to bring about change. And yet he also calls us to remember that we must maintain the purity of heart that can only come about as we contemplate God.

In contemplation, we remember that even the fight we fight for justice is temporary. There will come a day when there will no longer be a need to fight, to protest, to speak truth to power. For our whole identity to be wrapped up even in the fight for a better world is another form of dehumanisation. Learning to contemplate is therefore an act of asserting who we are first and foremost – children of God in whom God delights.

## Questions for reflection

1 Abba Moses can be considered an unlikely figure to be called by God because of his complex background. Do you identify with him because of this? Who in your context would fit into this group?

2 In your own spiritual practice, do you lean more towards the example of Mary or of Martha? What might you learn from the other?

3 When and where are the spaces you find (or might find) it easier to enter into contemplation? While you might not be able to leave your life to enter the desert, are there moments you might pinpoint for a retreat from the busyness of your life?

# Out of silence

Hopefully, in what I have said so far, it is clear that contemplation is not a kind of naval gazing, especially within Black spirituality and faith. Contemplation that turns our hearts and minds towards God will often involve us desiring to respond to God's love and grace, especially in relation to our neighbours. Where contemplative spirituality becomes self-centred or disconnects us from our neighbours and the world God loves, this says more about the contemplator than contemplation itself.

Contemplating God is an end in itself, a holy task that should not be instrumentalised or considered 'useless' if it does not lead to some external action. But neither should we be comfortable with only being concerned with personal piety as long as sin, death and violence undermine the life-giving work of the Spirit in our world. Revd Dr Howard Thurman, who was a spiritual advisor to Martin Luther King Jr, presents a good example of holding this tension together. He knew full well the problems that shaped his world, the Church and human lives. As an African American ordained pastor, theologian and civil rights activist, he was keen to encourage people to attend to their inner life even as they sought to make the world a better place. He compels us to give room to contemplation. For Thurman, contemplative spirituality was a stillness and quiet in which a person would be formed and moulded so that they might enter into the world as God intended. Our contemplation should compel us, ultimately, to greater love, which is not mere sentiment but committed action. Thurman reminds us:

> It is out of silence that all sounds come; it is in the stillness that the word is fashioned for the meaning it conveys. Here the sound without sounds can be most clearly heard and meanings out of which all values come can be plumbed.[1]

Silence described in this way might remind us of the very beginning of the Scriptures, which read, 'In the beginning God ...' I imagine this was a particularly quiet time, apart from the fluttering of the Spirit over the deep. And then, out of the silence, God's words come: 'Let there be ...' The pattern of sound coming out of silence in our own spiritual practices and lives is somewhat reminiscent of the way God's own voice came out of silence right at the beginning of creation. In fact, all of the sounds – of trees blowing in the wind, of frogs splashing in water and of birds squawking – emerge out of silence and follow the sound of God's command.

Silence, when thought about in such terms, is not an end point but a beginning. Silence is where we begin, as we come to our moments of prayer and contemplation. Prayers, hopes and intercessions may rise up in our consciousness as we take time to be silent. But it is also in this space that the Spirit, who is spoken of as a great intercessor, can pray with us and for us (Romans 8:26–7). The Spirit, who through 'wordless groans' prays for us, might even bring sounds out of our silence. In the place of tarrying, where we quiet ourselves, we give room to the Spirit to move us and speak to us, and to give us the grace to respond. Contemplative action can be the outcome – that our activity, our relationships and our work are enlivened by the Spirit who leads us from the place of stillness.

# 6

# Healing

Within Black spiritualities, healing and wellness are of great importance. Since, as we saw in chapter 2, all of life is recognised as integrated, rather than being opposed, all of life is expected to benefit from the life of God. The body and the spirit or soul must work together rather than being considered to be in conflict. This is especially important if we hope to have a healthy relationship with all aspects of who we are as human beings. Health is therefore holistic.

But health and healing is not an individual affair. In traditional African religions, wellness is understood to depend upon many factors. Health is not simply about the body being well; it is also social, spiritual, environmental, economic. Wellness depends upon one's relationship with the divine, with the earth and natural resources; it depends on one's connection to ancestral history, and on relationships with family and the wider community. This deeper understanding of health opens up broader understandings of sickness and healing, which are better aligned with what we find in the biblical text.

## The bleeding sister

The healing ministry of Jesus can be difficult to handle. In some charismatic contexts, stories of Jesus healing can become the main emphasis of preaching and spiritual practice. These stories are used to encourage people to believe that the Spirit of Christ who is present today is also able to heal. There are countless people who will testify to having received healing through prayer. This can also be true in contexts that might not label themselves as charismatic but might be open to God's healing in a range of ways. Here the emphasis might be less on physical healing, but a more holistic expectation that emotional hurt or relationships might be healed through prayer as well as other means.

Yet there are others who consider these biblical stories to simply be oral traditions that probably do not have much real impact on our current lives and experiences. Some might outright deny that God can or does heal, and simply imagine that those claiming to have been healed have experienced a kind of placebo effect.

Healing stories can be difficult and triggering for those of us who have believed that God could or even would heal, and then were disappointed. In some cases, we might worry that people will get their hopes up and will then have to deal with disappointment if healing doesn't happen. It can seem easier to avoid the question altogether. However, in a world in which so many of us suffer from various kinds of health issues, whether physical or not, or are affected by illness, we cannot avoid these questions for long. Though we should tread with caution, the biblical text does help us to think about healing and wellness in ways that can be helpful.

In order to think this through, I want to draw our attention to one particular story. Often these stories centre on one individual but have a ripple effect that can be felt in the wider community. The fact that we are still reading these stories proves how important they are in the collective imagination of the Church. They reach us through time and space. The story I want to examine is found in Mark 5:24–34 and Luke 8:43–8. It is the story of the woman with the haemorrhage; other versions call her 'the woman with the issue of blood'. The fuller version in the Gospel of Mark reads:

A large crowd followed and pressed around [Jesus]. And a woman was there who had been subject to bleeding for twelve years. She had suffered a great deal under the care of many doctors and had spent all she had, yet instead of getting better she grew worse. When she heard about Jesus, she came up behind him in the crowd and touched his cloak, because she thought, 'If I just touch his clothes, I will be healed.' Immediately her bleeding stopped and she felt in her body that she was freed from her suffering.

At once Jesus realised that power had gone out from him. He turned around in the crowd and asked, 'Who touched my clothes?'

'You see the people crowding against you,' his disciples answered, 'and yet you can ask, "Who touched me?"'

But Jesus kept looking around to see who had done it. Then the woman, knowing what had happened to her, came and fell at his feet and, trembling with fear, told him the whole truth. He said to her, 'Daughter, your faith has healed you. Go in peace and be freed from your suffering.'

I have heard this preached many times as a story of Jesus' power. He is wandering through the crowds, on the way to heal Jairus' daughter. He is not recorded as looking around to heal people, or even being aware of anyone in the crowd who needs healing. And yet it happens, without him even trying. In most cases when Jesus heals someone, there is a moment when he asks, 'What do you want me to do for you?' (Matthew 20:32), and the people say, for example, 'We want our sight,' and then Jesus opens their blind eyes. Or at times there is a slightly unusual approach, such as spitting in dirt to make mud (John 9:6). But every now and then we come across a story that is even less predictable. In a similar way to the man whose friends lower him through the roof to get him in front of Jesus (Mark 2:3–5), or the Syro-Phoenician woman who negotiates for her daughter's healing (Mark 7:24–30), this story is as much about this woman's determination as it is about the power of Jesus.

Healing does not fall into her lap; it is passing by, and she has to be ready to grab it.

But before we get to the miracle and what that means, we should, I think, take a step back. This story starts with some quite horrific details. Many of them might be missed by those who have never had regular periods, but for those of us who do or have, we can more easily imagine what this might mean. I imagine Mark, sitting down with the woman after she has experienced her healing, asking her the details for his records. Maybe they sit under the shade of a tree, or maybe she is so happy to be able to stand upright and feel the energy coursing through her body that she can't keep still. Either way, Mark asks her, 'So, tell me about your sickness.'

She might have suffered unbearable cramps, which if she was ever doubled over in pain would have drawn attention. But maybe her illness was not visible for the most part, and she might have been able to keep it to herself. How did she feel to talk about it? Were there other women around to make it easier? Of course, there were undoubtedly similar cultural issues to those that exist in so many contexts today, where menstruation, menopause and other aspects of women's health are not supposed to be talked about with men, or at the very least create embarrassment if they are. How does she tell Mark what was wrong? Does she blush, or beat around the bush, or maybe it is possible that she just comes out and says it – after all, it is now over!

She tells Mark that she suffered this bleeding and was not able to access the healthcare she needed. She explains that she spent all her money on visits with doctors, who made her worse. She tells him that she was driven into poverty and was still sick, and she was also ostracised from the social networks that should have been able to support her. She breaks the stigma in telling this man what happened so we can all read about it way after she has gone on to rest with her ancestors.

## Health issues

As I think about this woman's story, I remember the many people in our communities who live with illness or disabilities, and are driven into poverty. I think of those who spend so much of their money trying to access a timely diagnosis, or wait so long for an NHS appointment that they risk dying of their illness. I think of the many women who have been labelled as 'hysterical' when they have been in great pain, or those who have been ignored rather than being taken seriously. I remember the lack of investment in women's healthcare, and the struggle for basic monitoring and checks that could prevent long-term health issues. This woman represents many other Black women, who are almost four times as likely to die in childbirth in Britain, because too many assume we can stand more pain than white women, since we are not as 'feminine'.[1] I wonder how many women have their health mishandled, especially by men who do not understand them, to the extent that they are left in a worse position than when they started. I remember Belly Mujinga, the transport worker with pre-existing health issues, who died after being deliberately coughed and spat on by a customer who knew he had the Covid-19 virus.[2]

Taking these health justice issues seriously is part of what it might mean for us to engage with healing ministry in our day and time. As members of Christ's body, we might think about preaching the gospel, or about justice and reconciliation, as part of our calling. We might assume that healing must involve praying for individual bodies, but how often do we think about our role in channelling healing in communal forms? How does this fit in?

Nigerian biblical scholar Ruth O. Oke also asks us to consider this story of the woman with the 'issue of blood' in light of the stigmatisation of those living with HIV/AIDS.[3] In her mind, there are parallels to the ways women who bled were considered impure and ostracised in the ancient Jewish context, and the ways those living with HIV/AIDS and their families are treated today around the world. Both share 'issues of blood':

> The flow of blood as a result of childbearing and menstruation is termed impurity according to the ceremonial law of worship that pervades the OT era. She is perpetually segregated and cannot associate with others in the open (see Leviticus 15:13). This may have psychological effect on her because she is not allowed to interact with other members of her household or community … People living with HIV/Aids (PLH) are encountering the same manner of treatment as the woman with the issue of blood (WIB) from neighbours, colleagues and even family members … The [antiretroviral] drug cannot do the magic of keeping the ill [in] good health, but the goodwill, care and support from people coupled with the drug can do wonders.[4]

I was not yet alive when people first began to be aware of the problem of HIV/AIDS. But I would later learn about the way HIV/AIDS was allowed to end the lives of so many gay men in particular, in the UK and elsewhere. The lack of interest in researching the virus and informing and protecting communities at risk was testament to the hatred, fear and ambivalence people had towards gay people at the time, which has not ended, of course. I would later learn about the levels of HIV/AIDS across the African continent. Here again, the vulnerable suffer and are often considered expendable, as rumours abound about how people get infected and how it can be cured. The stigma can still prevent honest and open conversations, education and access to the necessary resources to help.

We do not hear much about HIV/AIDS in the UK, though it remains an epidemic of significant proportions around the world. In the latest data from the World Health Organization, an estimated 40 million lives have been lost to HIV so far, that we know of. And

40 million are living with the virus.[5] While there is no cure, drugs are now available that allow people to live full lives, if they happen to be in a country that has affordable access to them. Despite drugs being available, the poorest rarely have access, and death rates are increasing in some parts of Africa while declining elsewhere.

'Issues of blood' continue to shape the lives of so many, leading to isolation and death. There is often no healing available for those who suffer.

But in the biblical passage, the woman has an option. On one particular day, she sees the rabbi in the crowd and has an idea. There is no mention of anyone who has accompanied her; she seems to be alone, isolated from her friends and family. Or maybe she has sneaked out to go to where she has heard Jesus will be, since technically she should not be out and about owing to her 'impurity'. But since she has already lost everything, she has nothing more to lose.

She has enough strength to push her way through the crowd, but somehow can only reach the edge of his cloak. She tells herself that is all she needs really, since healing radiates from this person. Someone even said that his word alone is enough to heal someone.

As she holds on to his cloak, he stops and turns, almost catching her eye. 'Who touched me?' Jesus is used to being the one people ask for a healing touch or a healing word. But rarely does someone have the audacity to just grab his cloak. People are jostling, of course, and may even be grabbing his cloak in order to talk to him or just be close. But there is something different here. This woman believes. Her body is weak but her faith is strong. She receives exactly what she needs, and they have not even had a conversation about it. She is able to get what she needs from Jesus, and he doesn't even see her face. I imagine Jesus almost being shocked by this, as we might be when a person does something audacious – risky but bold.

The disciples don't understand how he could be asking this, but the woman knows why. She has felt something change in her, and so has he. She has even changed Jesus. I can see why she would be trembling, but she is met with gentleness. He calls her 'daughter' and sets her heart at ease. She is safe here and will not be condemned. Jesus, it seems, appreciates a woman who knows what she wants. She does not wait for permission or submit to those who would tell her to stay home in isolation – she advocates for herself and her health.

As I ponder this, I wonder about the depth and holistic nature of the healing she experiences. Yes, she has a physical health issue, and she really does want her bleeding to stop. We find she has done everything she can to address her illness, which is debilitating. This is a fair and understandable response. But I also wonder, why is she alone? Though Jesus has healed her body, I wonder how she is beyond the physical. Has she also been healed from the years of trauma she has suffered emotionally, socially, psychologically? We might hope so, and clearly she will now be able to participate in the community in ways she would not have been able to before. There is a social element to what it means for her to be healed.

As I ponder her determination, I ask whether her healing began even before she touched the robe. Was God working in her to get her to this point, where she was willing to venture beyond the limits of tradition to fight for her own life? Did her healing begin as she began to recognise that her life mattered, and that she deserved to be well? Or when she decided to break religious protocol to get what she needed from God, no matter the cost? She was healed in part, I think, from the debilitating thought that there was no future for her, no community of which she could ever be a part, and that God did not see her or care. Her mind and spirit were healed enough so that her body might also be.

This interaction between Jesus and this woman helps us to imagine what it means for those of us who call ourselves Christians to be part of this healing ministry. It involves allowing those who suffer to advocate for themselves and name what they need to be well. It includes making healing accessible so that those in need know where to go, and those in poverty are not forgotten. It also means recognising above all that those who suffer are family to us, worthy of welcome and not of condemnation, shame and judgement.

## Questions for reflection

1 What are your own reflections on the woman with the issue of blood? Do you see her as someone to be pitied or admired, or a mix of both?

2 Do your own understandings or experiences of healing focus on the physical or do they have a more holistic emphasis? What differences does this make to your ability to recognise 'sickness'?

3 In your own context, who are the groups whose health and wellness are most notably at risk? Who are the stigmatised? How does this story affect how you reflect on these groups?

# Healthy community

In this case, the woman has an illness. She recognises it as such, and wants to be healed. She is fortunate that she has access to healing as Jesus walks by. But there are many kinds of illnesses that cannot be cured, or are not cured even if there is a chance they could be. We cannot speak about such biblical accounts without acknowledging this fact. There are some kinds of health issues or disabilities that we learn to live with, because either our own bodies are affected or the body or bodies of those we love. If we have not had to deal with such a scenario yet, we probably will in the future, owing to age if nothing else. Those who do not have the option of healing have a lot to teach us about how we face what we cannot fix in life, even when we want to.

I have only ever ticked 'no' when asked on a form whether I have a disability. And yet, in light of what I have seen in my own family, I know that this may only be a temporary reality for me. I have family members who live and have lived with long-term health issues, and who would have identified as living with a disability. My mother had cancerous spinal tumours that left her unable to care for herself in any way for a period of time, and my grandmother now lives with dementia. These experiences have changed me as much as anything I have read on the topic. They have pushed me to explore the questions of who we are and what makes us human, when the bodies that are our homes begin to change and even threaten our very lives. They have forced me to consider how to live with the things we cannot change or heal.

Though this story of the woman with the issue of blood focuses on this individual woman and her mainly physical need, as I have said, healing can and *should* be considered in broader ways. Sickness and healing involve so many factors that we can overlook. We can focus too much on the physical body as a measure of health. A person who looks physically well (whatever we think that means) may have long-term health issues others do not notice, including mental health challenges. A person who lives with a physical limitation might live a rich and wonderful life because of the way they are included and loved by those they work with and live with. The problem is not the body itself, but the way a person is received or excluded because of it.

It is in this point that the connection between disability theology and Black faith and spirituality is most apparent. In the case of racism and ableism, people are categorised because of their bodies as 'not belonging' or somehow needing to be 'fixed'. Assumptions are made about what a person is capable of, whether they are valuable or useful or what they might be lacking. Both the person living in a world shaped by racism or the one affected by ableism (and of course many are affected by both or more) live in a world that is dominated by narratives about their inferiority. Restrictions are placed on the spaces they might inhabit, and too often places are rendered inaccessible because of the failure to recognise difference as a gift to us all.

When we believe humans *should* have certain physical or mental capacities, we – even inadvertently – speak of or treat those who are different as 'broken'. In theological terms, we might think that God intends for us as human beings to have a particular kind of body or mind, or to be able to do certain things. We think that God intends a particular type of life for each of us, in which we experience perfect (or generally good) physical health. Our spiritual practices themselves can depend upon certain health-related assumptions. John Swinton, in his work on dementia, asks:

> If finding God requires that we actively seek after God, then those who can no longer remember what it might mean to do so find themselves trapped in a place of eternal lostness and hopelessness. If we cannot seek the Lord, how can we praise God? If we cannot know and praise God, then how can our

hearts be anything other than restless? If then, as Anselm in like vein suggests, faith has to do with seeking understanding – that is, 'an active love of God seeking a deeper knowledge of God' – then it is clear that people with advanced dementia have no real way of finding God. The experience of seeking understanding is precisely what is being lost as one encounters the latter stages of the process of dementia.[1]

Sickness is considered an enemy, because it opposes what we imagine is needed for a good life. This includes the spiritual life, as Swinton touches on above. In the Bible we come across moments in which Jesus heals people and casts out demons that are linked to mental or physical illness. In the new heaven, we read that there will be no more sickness, no more dying (see Revelation 21:4). We imagine Adam and Eve to look, move and think like perfect human beings, an image we will all come to experience in heaven.

But where do we really get these ideas from about what bodies should be like and be able to do in order to be considered fully human? Why do we imagine that God can only meet us or we can only be disciples if we have particular capacities? It seems that these ideas are often rooted in our cultural norms, which demand that above everything a person should be able to go out to work, make money and look after themselves. Bodies that can participate in this norm are considered good and normal. Other bodies are considered a problem.

Whether because of disability, health issues, age or other factors, certain people are treated as if they are simply 'in the way'. We cannot imagine what will happen if a child is born with a long-term health issue or a partner or friend develops one – we worry for their future and our own. Our culture does not have a place for them. We fear their lives will change for the worse since our sense of a 'good life' is dominated by ideas of participation in the cycle of producing and consuming. Where does a person fit if they cannot play this role?

## Beyond individual healing

When I lay out the problems of health and well-being in this way, it should be clear, I hope, that health is a collective project, and so is healing. We can fixate on the person who has the illness or who lives with a physical or mental difference as the problem. In other words, the person who does not fit what we think of as 'well' or 'normal' is considered a problem to be resolved. But often, the problem is that their participation in community life is being prevented owing to the lack of adaptation by that community. What happens if we consider the ways the wider community, rather than the individual, is proving itself to be deficient or lacking?

If a healthy community, in light of the healing ministry of Jesus, is willing to shift the dynamics to embrace the person who has a health issue or is living with a disability, then are our communities healthy? Does the person need healing or does the community? Those of us presumed to be healthy often prove ourselves to be 'sick' in our lack of response to those living with illness or with mental or physical differences. We demonstrate impatience, a lack of care and concern, disregard and an absence of love that is a symptom, I think, of a deeper problem of our collective heart.

Disability theologians have greatly helped us to think better about what it means to go beyond individual healing, from a Christian perspective. Theologian Amos Yong, whose brother was born with Down syndrome, writes about an alternative view to the expectation that our response to disability should always be to seek for it to be eradicated. As a Pentecostal theologian, this was emphasised in his own tradition, but he has now come to see things differently:

People with Down Syndrome ... do not need to be cured; like all other people, however, they do need to be loved. To be sure, in some cases, curing precedes healing, such as when lepers are cleansed (or when demoniacs are delivered) precisely in order to facilitate restoration to their communities. Yet, in the parable of the great dinner, the crippled, blind, and lame are invited and included just as they are. Our focus, then, should be on how Jesus' ministry makes people whole.[2]

Jesus, of course, constantly asked people what they wanted from him; he never assumed. Maybe he understood this point too. Living with a long-term health issue or a mental or physical difference is not a barrier to God being present with us, even if our own notions of agency might be undone. When our understanding of our spiritual lives depends heavily on what we can do in the way Swinton describes, we can struggle to imagine what happens when we cannot perform as we think we should. Living with an illness can mean we have opportunities to experience God in ways that evade us when we do not. I would not say God has given people illness for this purpose, as some would. But I do believe that, if and when we experience these things in our lifetimes, they do not have to represent the end of our faith. We may well hope and pray for healing. And we might also, or instead, ask for the grace to be kept close to God as we walk that path.

For my nan, who does not always remember who I am even as she offers me a warm smile, she continues to abide in the love of God in whose arms she has rested her whole life. She can, on a good day, remember a few words of Psalm 23, in between questions about when my late grandfather is coming back from the shops. And she may even hum along to a worship song she hears on the radio, before she loses all sense of where she is. She is to me a reminder that, when all is said and done, and when nothing much can be said or done, I am a beloved child of God, who looks at me, smiles and says, 'You are my good creation.'

## Questions for reflection

1 To what extent are your reflections on disability shaped by assumptions about how a human being 'should' be? Where do those ideas come from for you?

2 How does thinking about God relating to those living with dementia shape your own ideas regarding how God is present to you?

3 Is the perspective of accepting rather than healing disability something that resonates with you? How might it shape how you handle challenging life circumstances in general, as a disciple of Jesus?

# Shared pain

So far we have thought about individual bodies, individual health and healing, recognising that it depends on the community. But it is also important to reflect on the pain and trauma that communities can carry as a whole, and the way this can be experienced even generationally.

If we begin again with the woman with the issue of blood, we might consider how this story works on a communal level. The individual stories we read of Jesus healing are, I think, a good indication of the collective possibilities opened up by God becoming flesh and living among us. So, yes, it is a story in which we can imagine how God may have responded or might now respond to our personal hurts, physical or otherwise. But we might also imagine what this could mean for the pains we share together. This woman might represent communities as a whole who struggle to get the healthcare they need and are driven into poverty by their ailments, or women from global majority backgrounds who have worse health outcomes then their white counterparts.

Jesus, in his body, words and actions, shows us a way of being with God and with one another that leads to life in all its fullness (see John 10:10). This is not just an individual message but a collective invitation. It is what is meant by the kingdom or reign of God. The reign of God is shown to us as Jesus demonstrates what God is seeking to invite us into as a human family. His actions are windows into something the people of his time could not even imagine: the promise that God is reconciling all people and creation to Godself.

Healing, then, though focused on individuals many times in the Scriptures, can be understood as an indication that God desires the wellness of all creation and of all people. Wellness as I understand it is not to be confused with a cultural notion of perfection, in which we seek to maintain our youth, particular body weights and shapes, and so on, at all costs. Health and well-being, in theological terms, is the experience of living in harmonious communion with God and God's creation, including ourselves, other people and the natural world. This harmonious communion is dependent on consideration of the other, self-control, mercy and kindness, gentleness and patience, all that God is to us and enables us to become by grace. And yet this harmonious communion can often feel like a distant dream. We may see glimmers of this communion in moments of beauty or joy that we encounter even in the mundaneness of life, but, as a whole, as human beings, we are far from this collective wellness.

This is sadly true even in the Church and in Christian communities, where we tend to hope that, at least on some level, we might experience something of the beauty of this promised just and holy community. Our congregations bring together people who would often come together for no other reason. And yet they can also be places for shared pain for those who are excluded or given only a conditional welcome. Jarel Robinson-Brown speaks about the particular pain experienced by those who are both Black and LGBTQ+, owing to the ways the Church and its leaders often respond to them:

> It is this sense that grace must be earned that pushes Black LGBTQ+ folk to hide all the non-heteronormative parts of ourselves in an effort to win God's love, the Church's welcome and the pastor's favour who, even though they know and have preached on St Paul's words about us as human beings who 'have this treasure in clay jars' (2 Corinthians 4.7), spend all their time guiding us to focus miserably on the clay-ness of ourselves and negating all the treasure. It is through them that we come to learn the very opposite of grace, through those individuals and communities who fail to accept, embrace and love us as God loves us.[1]

These pains are shared, often by groups within groups or between groups. In Black communities, Black LGBTQ+ people experience great harm, including in Black churches. In wider LGBTQ+ communities, Black people often face the same forms of racism and exclusion they do in wider white-majority society. Healing can, as I have already said, be harder to find for some.

Shared pain can also be present in the communal trauma that often goes unnoticed. The notion of intergenerational or communal trauma comes to the fore in the work of those researching the impact of the Holocaust on Jewish survivors and their descendants, as well as survivors of genocide and war in other contexts. For those of us who are descended from survivors of the transatlantic slave trade, it helps us to name and explore the harm that affects us, despite us not having been present at the time. We live with forms of ongoing trauma in what is and what is not. I live with a name that was given to me by Europeans who owned my ancestors as property. I do not know the language, location and culture of my African ancestors. My DNA reveals significant connections to Nigeria, Ghana, Ivory Coast and Benin, but also to Scotland, Norway and Ireland. This European ancestry is in all likelihood there not because of loving interracial relationships, but because of the rape of Black women by European men during their captivity. While there is much to explore with regard to research on trauma and Black communities, for many there is a feeling that something is not quite right. Christina Edmondson explains it this way:

> The past makes a claim on the present in our DNA. This impacts health outcomes throughout the life cycle and is a root cause to many adult health issues ... The trauma of my ancestors lives in my body today. I only need to walk by a mirror to be reminded of the sexual subjugation of Black women.[2]

Ben Lindsay has described the 'secondary trauma' that is experienced when, as Black people in the UK, we are faced with the 'continued bombardment' of online videos of those who look like us experiencing racial violence.[3] Practical healing work being done with communities affected by histories of trauma does suggest that a form of post-traumatic stress might be passed down intergenerationally. Those living under the threat of death over extended periods are believed by some to be negatively affected in body and mind. This, some imagine, can be inherited biologically and, if not processed and properly managed, can lead to health issues for individuals and the collective.[4] This should not reinforce any racist ideas that might victimise Black people or deny our agency, but it should give reason to think about how health might be affected by history and events that happen elsewhere, not just by our own individual choices and personal experiences today.

The impact of historic trauma is shared not only in physiological or psychological terms but also in ways that are cultural, economic, political and social. It would seem plausible that with 10–12 million Africans forcibly removed and enslaved, with millions more affected over several hundred years, this might have had a long-term impact on African and particularly African Caribbean communities. Likewise, can we imagine that colonial violence and subsequent wars in China, Bangladesh, Pakistan, India and elsewhere have had no lasting negative effects on individuals, families or communities? The spectre of colonial violence remains in laws, government policies, economic arrangements and social norms.

Generational trauma deserves our attention. Even when the dust is believed to have settled, the impact on minds and hearts lives on. Every act of racial violence or incidence of discrimination today triggers the memories of countless previous incidents, experienced personally or by those who look just like us. History lives on.

## Questions for reflection

1 When considering different groups in society, do you pay attention to their histories and the impact of communal trauma? How might this affect your understanding of those you consider to be different?

2 How alert are you to the ways different groups even within an overarching social group face additional forms of exclusion and harm (such as Black women, those who are Black and LGBTQ+, disabled or living in poverty?)

3 What might it take for you to cultivate greater awareness of these stories and experiences?

# Healing together

It is this shared trauma that, in part, puts healing front and centre in Black spirituality and faith. The depth of pain is understood to be something that God must act to address, even if one might also depend on therapists and counsellors, medication or protest. There is a spiritual wound that must be named. This is in part because the harm itself is often interpreted as having spiritual elements.

As people who often believe in 'demonic powers', there is arguably no clearer example than some of the organised forms of evil that plague Black lives in Britain. When Black children such as Child Q are illegally strip-searched by police without a parent or teacher present, and this is revealed to be motivated in part by racism,[1] it is understandable that some might call this 'demonic'. If police can chase and shoot dead Chris Kaba, instead of arresting and questioning him,[2] what other label can we give this but 'principalities and powers'?

When the terms 'demonic' or 'principalities and powers' are used to describe the manifestation of forces that are opposed to the life and goodness of God in creation, these interpretations are fair. This does not mean the only solution is to pray demonic activity away, though spiritual warfare does play an important part in opposing such evil for many. On the contrary, these spiritual readings of what takes place equip people filled with the Spirit to take a physical and spiritual stand in prayer and organised action.

Prayer and protest, therefore, work hand in hand within Black faith as mechanisms for healing together. Tarrying, as I have described already, can be understood as a space for healing, as we bring burdens, pains and woes to God. We hope, in this space, to gain 'beauty for ashes, the oil of joy for mourning, the garment of praise for the spirit of heaviness' (Isaiah 61:3, KJV). Prayers in whatever form, spoken by lips, repeated silently in one's heart or articulated through marching feet, are an avenue for intercession.

They give us the chance to name what ails us collectively and what needs to be healed.

Healing requires confession, a facing of what is wrong. It demands the courage to pull back the shredded clothing, take a good look at the wound and decide what needs to be done. And so it can be fearful work. We risk being overwhelmed by emotions, which we must grow to manage. While we might prefer a kind of positive spirituality, this often betrays an inability or immaturity regarding the need to tell the truth about the pain that so often marks our human experience. Cole Arthur Riley explains it this way:

> We will not heal divorced of our emotions. A spirituality that depends on positivity will lead not only to emotional fallacies but also eventually to delusions of all kinds. Hundreds of thousands of people can march for miles declaring Black Lives Matter, and you will find it so disruptive to your delusions of positivity that you will not become curious or sensitive. Instead, you will find yourself defensive of your fallacy.[3]

Healing depends, therefore, on our capacity to face the truth and tell the truth. It demands that we face the truth as revealed in the stories of those we do not want to listen to. It requires that we face the truth of our own actions (or inactions), which reveals the truth about our actual convictions and beliefs. Prayer is a space to lay down the fallacies we long to defend, and to ask God in Christ, and in the face of our neighbour, 'What must I do to be saved?' (see Acts 16:30).

Protest demonstrates a commitment to truth-telling, to witnessing to the evil, injustice and wrongdoing that occurs in the world. It is disruptive, as Riley describes, because it disturbs those who lead people astray, 'saying, "Peace", when there is no peace' (Ezekiel 13:10). In the same way that the people of Israel marched around the walls of Jericho, so too Black communities and their allies move their feet and are prepared to shout when the moment comes. The story in Joshua 6 reads as follows:

> So Joshua son of Nun called the priests and said to them, 'Take up the ark of the covenant of the LORD and make seven priests carry trumpets in front of it.' And he ordered the army, 'Advance! March round the city, with an armed guard going ahead of the ark of the LORD.'
>
> When Joshua had spoken to the people, the seven priests carrying the seven trumpets before the LORD went forward, blowing their trumpets, and the ark of the LORD's covenant followed them. The armed guard marched ahead of the priests who blew the trumpets, and the rear guard followed the ark. All this time the trumpets were sounding. But Joshua had commanded the army, 'Do not give a war cry, do not raise your voices, do not say a word until the day I tell you to shout. Then shout!'
> (Joshua 6:6–10)

This is a miraculous tale of the people of Israel gaining victory, not through violence – though they do resort to violence eventually, and to be clear, this should not be the moral of the story in my view – but through a peaceful march. They are led not by the warriors, but by the priests, those whose lives have been dedicated to the worship of God and the spiritual life of the people God has called. The presence of God goes ahead of them in the ark of the covenant and they march behind in silence, until the seventh time around.

Peaceful protest has been a core strategy for those steeped in the Christian tradition who are also concerned for Black lives. They teach us that being led by God's ways and God's person is crucial in the desire we have to heal the world. We know, from those who have gone before us, that we cannot resort to the same weapons that have done harm in an attempt to heal. If domination, force and violence have created the pain and trauma we hope to address, then we know we cannot use those same weapons to right those wrongs. The weapons of our warfare for *healing* cannot be 'carnal', but are 'mighty through God to the pulling down of strongholds' (2 Corinthians 10:4, KJV). They include the quiet inner work, our dependence on the Spirit, our determination to hold all things together and our commitment to leaving no person or group behind when we move.

As in the case with the story of Jericho, which gives Jewish communities a sense of rootedness in history, so knowing our history also provides important signposts for Black communities. The interruption of that history is part of the communal trauma I have been discussing. Delroy Hall, a counsellor and chaplain with many years of ordained ministry experience, speaks in *A Redemption Song* about a 'mass amnesia', whereby African Caribbeans have little or no knowledge of their history. In response, he asks what the psychological, emotional and existential consequences are for people who cannot lay claim to their history.[4] He reminds us of the reality that health and well-being also depend upon a healthy connection to history, and particularly to ancestral history. This is an important point for all of us. Our sense of identity is not created simply as we read the Bible, but also as we hear and interpret our wider history. This often involves the stories told to us by our parents, carers, families and wider community about who we are and where we have come from. We develop a sense of self as we hear about what we were like as babies or young people. But we also come to understand a bit more about where we belong, as we hear about those who have gone before us. There is a kind of healing that comes from learning about those who blazed trails, pushed boundaries and overcame the unthinkable. We can be healed as we identify such figures and also learn from them what it takes to heal a community.

I would like to consider the contemporary example of a person who has recently joined the realm of the ancestors: the Revd

Carmel Jones. During my PhD research, I interviewed his daughter Elaine and his grandson Shane to hear his story. Revd Jones was a Jamaican Anglican when he arrived in the UK at the age of seventeen and joined the Pentecostal Church of God in Christ when he was refused entry to his local Anglican church. Though this was a traumatising experience at the time, providentially, being located in a Black church meant that he came face to face with the predicaments being experienced by those in his community. Black people gathered together in front rooms for worship, and soon the congregations grew too big. They would then move to church halls, which they soon outgrew again. It was not long before they needed to buy whole buildings for their large congregations. Yet when they attempted to do so, they were refused access to loans. Not only this, but Black people were also being racially discriminated against when they went to apply for loans to buy houses.

Revd Jones founded the Pentecostal Credit Union (PCU) in the early 1980s as a solution to these problems. He was deeply concerned with the frustrations, oppression and injustice being experienced by his community and decided to do something about it. Revd Jones was a praying man, and when he saw an advert in a newspaper about starting a credit union, he realised this was what he had been praying for. He was also inspired by the civil rights movement in the USA in which Revd Dr Martin Luther King Jr, another ordained pastor, had been fighting for the rights of African Americans across the pond. He decided to launch a credit union in order to ensure that his community had access to affordable loans, to enable them to buy houses and churches. African Caribbeans had been used to informal arrangements known as *pardna* whereby they would pay into a shared pot and take it in turns to withdraw from it.

The credit union became a regulated organisation, and it remains one of the strongest credit unions to this day. The PCU has enabled thousands of people who would otherwise have been economically disenfranchised to develop financial stability and plan for their futures. The PCU has worked especially on financial education with young people, and has supported survivors of domestic abuse with the tools to build a new future for themselves and sometimes their children.

This story of courage and innovation illustrates to us the kind of action that enables healing and flourishing for communities that are living with ongoing trauma and forms of oppression. It is important in particular that we celebrate stories of innovation that come from within such communities. If part of the harm of a traumatic history is that one loses a sense of one's own self-worth, value and agency, then the path to healing must look different. There are, of course, important instances where allyship is required, but this should not overtake the healing that must take place within which allows a group to free themselves. The stories we tell about liberation, which are healing, should reinforce the idea that those with power must be trusted with the task of freeing those they have disempowered. This will only ever lead to partial freedom and incomplete healing.

## Questions for reflection

1 What are your responses to the idea that protest and prayer can work together? Can you see how protest might form part of a person's or a group's spiritual practice?

2 Are there individuals in your own history, or those you have heard of, who have enabled healing through their own creativity, innovation and determination? What do you learn from their example?

3 If healing is social, what kinds of communities do we need to create to enable well-being in the Church and in wider society?

# 7

# Weeping

In this final chapter, we will attend to the weeping that endures, sometimes for many nights, before joy comes with the morning (see Psalm 30:5). Here we will name some of the particular pains of Black communities, in the context of reflections on Jesus' final days and suffering during what is known as Holy Week. This week, which begins with Palm Sunday, captures the breadth of human experience, including many elements that shape Black life in particular. It is a week in which we come face to face with the fickleness of human beings – both ourselves and those we meet and with whom we share the world.

The crowds welcome Rabbi Jesus into Jerusalem, laying down their coats and palm branches in honour of his arrival. The disciples who know that Jesus has been reluctant to go into Jerusalem may wonder why, once they see this warm welcome. They may even assume that their messianic hopes will be fulfilled. Instead, in a matter of days, they are scattered, with Jesus facing the cross alone.

In this chapter, we are invited to ponder the contradictions that mark our own lives, as we walk with God and await life in its fullness. We are invited to give space to our own tears and those of our neighbours, as this is part of what it means to love. In the following sections, we will be able to see our own pains through the lens of Christ's own life, and the betrayal, torture and death he suffered. This week is the climax of what it means to tarry, to be in the in-between space between what we hope for and what is. It is the time when we sit with Jesus, awake in the darkness, as he asks, 'Could you not tarry with me, even for an hour?' (Matthew 26:40, my paraphrase).

# Disappointment

Disappointment is often the source of our grief and our weeping in this life. It is what we feel when we are faced with pain or problems we did not expect, when our hopes fall flat and the good we imagine does not come to pass. It is a thoroughly human experience, and one that is unavoidable. Disappointment can build up in our hearts and minds in a thousand tiny interactions: in the friend who stops calling, the partner who won't make an effort, the child who turns out to be more complicated than we feel prepared to handle, in the boss who turns out to be a bully. Sometimes we are able to name it and share the burden with someone else, and at other times we do not feel we can even admit it out loud.

But sometimes the disappointment we feel is self-inflicted. It is possible to let ourselves down through our own actions or inaction, in the past or the present. For some of us, this can be a great weight in our lives. We feel that we must strive to be good, and yet so often we miss the mark we set for ourselves. We hope to be loving, kind and gracious, but so often we are the opposite. We wish we had spoken up for that person or group, but we didn't, and we enabled harm to come to them. It may be something as simple as wishing we had checked on that person who looked lonely at church, or that we had called that person who crossed our mind. We feel disappointed that we cannot maintain the good habits we know will help us and resist the ones that will harm us and others. Disappointment is not something we only have to deal with when others let us down; it is also something we have to contend with within ourselves.

In addition, we are faced with disappointment in our churches and with the wider body of Christ. We feel collective disappointment every time a church leader is revealed to be a predator or an abuser. Christians arguing and fighting online, leaders who do not speak when it is hoped they will, others speaking and saying what is unhelpful, all trigger feelings of disappointment. Institutional failures with regard to safeguarding, racial justice or LGBTQ+ pastoral care, all send shockwaves through individuals and communities because of the hopes we tie to the Church and its leaders. The decisions of our government have heightened the sense of disappointment beyond the Church, in wider society as a whole. We might feel disappointed at the lack of action on climate change, the lack of moral example provided by leaders, the demonising of migrants and the failure to invest in public services. The hopes we have for a world of justice and peace can seem a long way off.

Disappointment can become a kind of 'death by a thousand cuts' for our faith. It is one of the undetected enemies of our spiritual lives. This is especially the case if we try to pretend we are not affected, instead of findings ways to process disappointment. We are used to naming doubt, maybe as a problem to be overcome or simply as an inevitable element of the journey of faith. We talk about temptation as something we must be on our guard against – temptations that come from within as well as those that come at us externally. But we rarely speak of disappointment.

For me, disappointment has posed and still poses one of the biggest threats to my life with God. This, I think, is one of the big failings of the kind of Christianity that many of us have inherited. A faith was advertised to us that would help our dreams to come true, and we bought it, sometimes with everything we had. We have not been prepared, through faith, for the moments when life becomes a nightmare. Our Christian faith can sometimes prepare us to hope and even to have our hopes fulfilled, but not for disappointment.

Most of us, even if we are not honest about it, live somewhere between hope and disappointment, or perhaps at a crossroads where they meet. We might be scared of telling the truth to ourselves. We may be afraid to admit that we can often be disappointed by God. Faith can be fragile, and telling the truth about disappointment can feel similar to lighting a match underneath a house of cards. We wonder, *Once I do this, will I be able to control or stop what happens?*

I can understand the fear. To be clear: God is not disappointing. God is the source and sustainer of life, complete in holiness and goodness. But the expectations we project on to God set us up for a depth of disappointment that many of us struggle to and never recover from.

Some of us have fallen, or now fall, into the camp of those we often refer to as 'deconstructing'. Deconstruction is for the disappointed, or at least for those ready to admit we are. It is a place where people say, 'I have been let down by this person or this community or this faith that I gave my life to or believed in with all my heart.' Maybe after a thousand small nudges, or one or two huge ones, the house came crashing down. Many of us discover that the very simple ideas shared in songs, sermons, prayers or conversations could not hold the weight of life in all its complexity and pain. There were no nuances, no what-ifs, no safety net, no explanations, just an encouragement to believe and not doubt. This might have felt comforting and attractive at one stage. Many have given their whole lives to God and the Church, because of how sincerely we believed. But then the disappointments started to stack up.

Jesus is aware of the danger of disappointment to our faith, and we can see him addressing it both for the crowds and for the disciples. The crowds are not those who have committed to following Jesus; they are simply intrigued by what they are seeing. They hang around him because they know he will meet some of their immediate needs for food or healing. But they are not sure about him; they do not have any strong conviction about who he is. But Jesus understands them, their disappointments and their hopes. In the famous Sermon on the Mount, he addresses them:

Blessed are those who mourn,
    for they will be comforted.
Blessed are the meek,
    for they will inherit the earth.

Blessed are those who hunger and thirst for righteousness,
  for they will be filled.
(Matthew 5:4–6)

In other words (in my paraphrase): 'I know you feel let down right now because you are mourning, and God's promise seems like a long way off, but it is not over yet. I know that in this world meek people get trampled on, and that fills you with disappointment because that isn't how it is supposed to be, but in the end you will inherit God's creation. I see that the state of the world is causing you to despair, but believe me, it isn't over; you will have what you hope for.'

With the disciples, his approach is different. These are the people he considers his friends, those who have said yes to his calling. Jesus is keen to ensure they understand what it is they have agreed to, and he prepares them for what lies ahead. The disciples meet Jesus with huge expectations for the restoration of Israel, and at the time many people are promising that they can deliver it. But Jesus spends so much of his time, and so many of his words, helping the disciples to reset their expectations. He knows they may be disappointed, but he wants them to understand what he is here for. When at the Last Supper in Luke 22 they start to argue about who is the worst and the best among them, he responds:

The kings of the Gentiles lord it over them; and those who exercise authority over them call themselves Benefactors. But you are not to be like that. Instead, the greatest among you should be like the youngest, and the one who rules like the one who serves. For who is greater, the one who is at the table or the one who serves? Is it not the one who is at the table? But I am among you as one who serves.
(Luke 22:25–7)

In other words (again my paraphrase), 'I know that you are expecting that when I say "kingdom" I mean a kingdom like the Romans. They have huge palaces and thrones, and dominate those they lead, treating them as if they are worthless. But I am doing something entirely different.' I imagine him saying, 'If you are following me thinking that in this life you are going to get thrones, crowns, wealth and status, you will be very disappointed. This is not what I am about. My kingdom is not of this world.' He warns the disciples, 'Don't be surprised (shocked and disappointed) if people persecute you because of me. If they do it to me, of course they will do it to you' (see Matthew 5:11, 24:9; John 15:20).

Jesus doesn't want them to be disappointed when the difficult times come. He does not want them to get tripped up in their faith, when following him leads in the opposite direction to what is valued and celebrated by the wider world. He wants them to understand that he is not building a new, glossier version of what they have seen others do; rather, he is doing something that has never been done before. 'The last will be first, and the first will be last' (Matthew 20:16). The righteous will be persecuted for his sake. He wants them to be prepared so that the disappointment does not rob them of their faith.

The week before Jesus' crucifixion is the ultimate test of the disciples' expectations and their capacity to handle disappointment. Jesus knows his death is coming and has sought to make this clear on many occasions (Matthew 16:21; Mark 8:31; Luke 9:22; 17:25). But it is one thing to hear this in theory, and another to live it. Jesus says to Peter, 'Satan has asked to sift all of you as wheat,' but then he says, 'I have prayed for you' (Luke 22:31–2).

## Questions for reflection

1  In what ways do you experience disappointment?
2  How might you create space in your spiritual practice to acknowledge these feelings, whether alone with God or with the help of a friend or supportive person in your life?

# Coping with disappointment

The Gospel accounts of Jesus' last few days provide much to reflect on in terms of the theme of disappointment. The disciples' responses are interesting to examine. This is not for the purpose of judging ourselves – we cannot tell how we might act in our own moment of sifting. But we may begin to attend to what is present in our hearts, as we seek to walk faithfully with God, through what we discover from their examples. Jesus does not escape these feelings, as we see. He, too, is familiar with this aspect of our human experience.

## Judas

Judas is named frequently as the betrayer of Jesus, but he is, in broader terms, an opportunist who takes advantage of the situation. I wonder whether underneath his betrayal was disappointment that Jesus might not be the 'cash cow' he had hoped. Maybe he had imagined that being with Jesus would make him rich. We know that Judas was greedy and loved money. He is not recorded as being driven by any particular values – he was not a Zealot fighting for political liberation, for example – he just desired money. We read that Judas was helping himself to the money that was given to support Jesus (John 12:6), and so encouraged people to give more money for that reason. The religious leaders did not go to him, offering an opportunity to betray Jesus, but rather he sought them out. He specifically went to the chief priests, asking, 'What are you willing to give me if I deliver him over to you?' (Matthew 26:14–15).

In the end, Judas was 'filled with remorse' and tried to give back the silver he had earned. Maybe, in the end, he remembered how Jesus had loved him, and the laughter he had shared with the other disciples, and he was filled with regret. His love of money had deceived and distracted him, and it cost him everything. He was so disappointed in himself that he took his own life (Matthew 27:3–8).

Betraying Jesus to get rich is an old business. In every generation, the lust for wealth is waiting to oppose and undermine the message of Christ, if we allow it. Indulgences, wealth gained by the Church by trading in slaves and colonial exploitation, investment in destructive industries, the prosperity gospel: all are examples of attempting to serve both God and 'mammon' (Matthew 6:24, KJV). Judas reminds us that idolatry can lead us to disappointment. Our love for wealth, or indeed other pleasures, over God can mean that our life with God ceases to satisfy us. We may somehow imagine that being a disciple of Jesus is the path to wealth and material success, or maybe fame and status, or whatever else we hope for. We betray Jesus when, like Judas, we attempt to use Christ and his message to further our own self-centred ambitions. It is an act of idolatry in which we create God in our own image and seek to make God our servant. Our idols will ultimately let us down and lead us to death as our relationship with God and God's creation (including ourselves and others) is disordered.

## Peter

Peter is a friend of Jesus who denies him in the moment of testing. Peter is one of the faithful ones; he 'gets it', but he ends up doing something he never imagined he would. When Jesus tells Peter that he will deny him, Peter is offended and outright rejects any notion that this could be true. He has a clear idea of who he is: someone who will be with Jesus to the end. But then when the time comes, we see that he does in fact deny his friend Jesus. When the cock crows, he experiences deep disappointment in himself. He did not know what was in his own heart. And when he sees what is there, he breaks down and weeps bitterly (Mark 14:29–30, 66–72; Matthew 26:33–4, 69–75).

I am grateful for Peter's inclusion in the text, and even for his moment of weakness, which does not lose him his place in Jesus' love once Jesus comes back from the dead (John 21:15–19). His story demonstrates for us that the line between friend and enemy, believer and non-believer, faithful and unfaithful, can be a lot less clear than we might want to admit. Peter is a person of good intentions who is taken by surprise by his own response in a moment of pain and disorientation. Unlike Judas, he does not demonstrate a habit of deception and betrayal; this is unexpected.

The story of Peter should generate some humility in those of us who would describe ourselves as the 'faithful' who expect other people to be the ones who will deny Jesus, but never us. Rather than thinking we are better than Peter, we might instead be led to pray for mercy for our own moments of testing, which will reveal what we might not imagine lies within us. And we might be led to view with kindness those we see as denying Christ, whose tests and trials we do not know. For we may find ourselves weeping as we discover that we are capable of doing what might bring us shame when our own time of testing comes.

## Mary Magdalene and the women

Mary and the women are not named as being present at the Last Supper, or in Gethsemane, although we know they were among the disciples. But they are recorded as staying close enough to see what was happening to Jesus on the day of his crucifixion. As he hung on the cross, 'many women were there, watching from a distance' (Matthew 27:55–6; Mark 15:40–1). These women had followed him all the way from Galilee to care for his needs, and they refused to abandon him even then. Mary Magdalene, Mary the mother of James and Joseph, the mother of Zebedee's sons and Salome are all named. They watched him as he died, they followed the soldiers as they brought his body to the tomb of Joseph of Arimathea, and they sat outside the tomb to guard him. They wept bitterly on that day, I imagine, though for different reasons from those of Peter. Yet their disappointment does not drive them away.

Mary Magdalene had already had her life transformed by Jesus. She was not one of the disciples who was fine going about their lives before their encounter with Jesus. While many were simply working, having families and living healthy lives, she was possessed by seven demons on the day Jesus crossed her path (Luke 8:2). Drawn to this rabbi, who treated women with dignity and respect, she and the other women had committed their lives and resources to supporting him and his ministry. They listened to him, hanging on his every word as he painted a picture of the life he was guiding them towards. They heard him speak about what lay ahead, including his own death, and when it arrived they were prepared. They understood that the temple would be torn down, but then it would be rebuilt, and so for that, they tarried.

## Jesus

Jesus is the one whose suffering is most obvious to us in Holy Week. Though we talk about him as fully human in theory, we often do not think much about his human responses to what he endured. I hear the disappointment in the question he asked of his friends: 'Could you not tarry with me for one hour?' I wonder what Jesus felt after he finished praying in the garden, and he saw the torches as the chief priests and guards approached.

He had prayed, asking God to 'take this cup from me' (Mark 14:36), even as he ultimately affirmed his willingness to endure what he must. Did his heart sink as he realised that there was no way for this 'cup' to pass him by? Did he hope all the way through the trial, the whipping, the mockery, that maybe he would still be spared? When he cried out, 'My God, my God, why have you forsaken me?' (Matthew 27:46), was that the moment he realised that God would not save him from his torturous death? Was that when the depth of his disappointment broke his heart?

I know many of us may not like to think of Jesus like this. It is unnerving. But I think Jesus' own disappointment – which,

I humbly imagine, he may have felt to some degree – may have been couched to some extent by his expectations. The anguish of disappointment is as deep as the height of one's hope. The greater the joy we attach to a particular outcome, the deeper the pain when it does not happen or seems out of reach. Jesus, I think, had one hope: that God would hold all things, even this, and make it right. His expectation was purely that God whom he knew and with whom he was one would ultimately ensure that life and love would win over sin and death. That divine power, which is seen in divine love, would not give way to violence, destruction and evil. This was his hope, and this hope, he knew, would never betray him. He knew that Peter would deny him – he did not have high expectations and was thus not disappointed. He knew what was in the hearts of the crowd so did not 'entrust himself to them' (John 2:24). He even expected the religious leaders to try to kill him – his soul was not crushed by disappointment in this regard. But maybe he was disappointed by his friends, and even by the reality that God would not spare him this pain, even, as the writer of the letter to the Hebrews suggests, for the sake of the 'joy set before him' (Hebrews 12:2).

## Questions for reflection

1 Does the love of money, or something else, lead you to betray Jesus or his message in your own life?

2 How do you process any disappointment you may feel with yourself or others? How might you find ways to practise kindness and grace in response?

3 What do you learn from Mary Magdalene and the women disciples about remaining steadfast when life becomes difficult?

# Tarrying with Mary, mother of the Crucified

The year after my mum died of cancer at the age of fifty-four, I decided to take a solo trip. I had several places in mind for holidays with some great future love: Venice and Rome were both on the list. And since, as I had recently discovered, life was full of unexpected horrors, I decided that I had better get a move on, even if that meant going alone.

I found one of those holiday packages where you can visit multiple places at once, and asked my friends who knew Rome well where I would find good food and the best sites. And off I went. My friend Father Simon had suggested a few churches, including the Basilica of San Clemente, which had an archaeological site in the crypt of one of the earliest churches in the city. Walking on this sacred ground was an unforgettable experience. As I went outside to continue my explorations, it suddenly started to rain very heavily. Giving up my carefully planned schedule, I ran around a corner looking for shelter and found another church (this is very common in Rome). This seemed a lot less busy, not many people were there and it was a haven from what was at this point torrential rain.

As I shook off some of the water that had drenched me and tried to look as though I had planned to be there, I looked to my left and saw a painting that gripped me. In it, I saw a figure holding the body of Jesus which had just been taken down from the cross. I walked closer to get a better look; it was Mary who was holding him. I sat down in silence. As I stared at this picture, I felt myself being drawn into the scene. I wanted to comfort Mary and tell her how sorry I was that this had happened. Her face was full of agony and grief.

It wasn't long before I realised that my urge to comfort her was linked to my own desire to be comforted. It was nine months since I had held my mum's body in the hospital on the night she died. I had held her on many occasions before that, as her carer. As the cancerous tumours had prevented her from being able to sit down, get up or stand without assistance, I had lifted, supported and laid her body down more times than I could remember.

I sat there, pondering Mary's pain and my own, and the bodies of those we loved, and in that moment I no longer felt alone. I felt Mary. I did not hear a sound or conjure up something from my imagination. I felt, in a spiritual way that could not be explained, that she was present with me. I felt that she understood what I felt, though it had not been my child, but my mother I had watched die slowly, over not hours but weeks. I felt the power of her motherly love reach out to me, as powerfully as my own mother's love continued to hold me even after her death.

I could not and still cannot really explain this experience; I was not brought up to think very much about Mary. For me, Mary was someone Roman Catholics considered to be of great importance, but in my own tradition she was simply a vessel for the bringing of Jesus into the world.

When I came back to England, I called one of my best friends, Ana, who is a Roman Catholic from Brazil. I explained what I had experienced, and she was not fazed at all – to her, it made total sense. I was glad one of us felt this way. She began to explain the importance of the Mary in Catholicism, their belief that she is alive and with Jesus and is someone they can speak to in prayer. As the saints who are part of the 'great cloud of witnesses' (Hebrews 12:1) who are not truly dead but only absent in the body, we might continue to communicate with them and ask for their prayers. This is not the same as praying to God, but is a way of recognising our connection to a community of saints that transcends time and space. This theology, which was not emphasised in this way as I was growing up, has enabled me to maintain a sense of spiritual connection with my mum, and the ancestors who have gone ahead of me. It has been invaluable to the strengthening and deepening of my faith.

Though Mary has not always been an important figure in the Protestant spiritual landscape in which I grew up, she has always been a significant person for me personally. As a young woman who felt called by God but was also from the wrong part of town, I resonated with her. This young woman was brown, I later discovered, like my own skin was. She loved God and was willing to play her role in the outworking of God's will in the world.

I would later discover that womanists and feminists also thought about Mary a lot, often for similar reasons. Mary in our reflections can often be presented as a meek, obedient, 'good girl' who said yes to God and did not doubt. This has often been weaponised against women, to mean that women must always be obedient when God or 'men of God' require or demand something from them. Mary is presented as not resisting, not debating, not questioning, and this is held up as a good example for women in particular. The ground is laid for abuse and violation, for ignoring questions of consent, and for denying women's dignity and voice when we allow this image and these theologies to prevail.

Roman Catholic womanist Diana Hayes discusses the particular importance of recognising Mary's agency and strength, not solely her obedience:

Black Catholics also speak a new and challenging word about Mary, the mother of God, rejecting the symbol of passivity for the courageous and outrageous authority of a young unwed mother who had the faith in herself and in her God to break through the limitations her society placed upon her in order to say a powerful yes to God, standing alone yet empowered. Hers was not a yes to being used merely as a passive, empty vessel, but a yes to empowerment, challenging the status quo by her ability to overcome those who doubted and denied her and to nurture and bring forth her Son as a woman of faith and conviction. The image of Mary and the infant Jesus is an image of strength and courage, of a mother's determination to bring forth this child regardless of the circumstances and conditions opposing her, a situation in which many Black women have often found themselves.[1]

Mary's 'yes' begins a journey that culminates in Holy Week, in the death of her son. She is a mother, like many who lose their children to violence, sometimes at the hands of those in power, sometimes at the hands of those who are equally disempowered. As I ponder Mary, I remember the mothers for whom the death of their children has also been public or made public. I think of Baroness Doreen Lawrence, who has fought tirelessly and courageously for justice for her son Stephen. I remember Mina Smallman, the mother of Bibaa Henry and Nicole Smallman, who has continued to fight for justice after police officers created and shared selfies with the corpses of her two murdered daughters. I think of the mother of Sabina Nessa, the teacher murdered in London, whose face has appeared many times on the news, as she debates how the justice system can better address violent acts. So, too, the mothers of many more killed in the UK: Mark Duggan, Dea-John Reid, Sarah Everard, Chris Kaba, Elle Edwards, Olivia Pratt-Korbel and those whose deaths are not considered newsworthy.

Mary, like many of us, lived a life of joy mixed with sorrow, and faith intertwined with disappointment, grief born out of love. I wonder whether Mary felt any disappointment or whether she, like Jesus, had an inclination of what might happen. The prophet Simeon, on the day Jesus was presented in the temple, warned Mary that 'a sword will pierce your own soul too' (Luke 2:35). We read that Mary pondered what was happening with Jesus, and 'treasured all these things in her heart' (Luke 2:51). Did she imagine things would turn out in the way they did? I wonder if she ever spoke to Jesus and warned him to calm it down a bit because of the risks he faced? Was she anxiously praying that God would protect him and preserve his life, or simply that he would have the courage to do God's will? Did she look back over her prophetic song, the Magnificat, in Luke 1 and wonder, what on earth has come of this?

It would seem during this time that rejoicing is impossible, and she is cursed and not blessed. In this Holy Week, the humble are scattered rather than the proud, and rulers sit comfortably on their thrones. In this moment, it seems that the humble are being crushed, not lifted up; the hungry hunger still for what is good, while the greed of the rich knows no end. It seems as if God has forgotten to be merciful to Abraham's descendants, and has in fact broken God's own promise.

We find Mary at the foot of the cross, on which Jesus is hung and dying (John 19:25). I can only imagine her weeping. Weeping because her son has suffered torture and death that we cannot comprehend. Weeping because her husband is not there to comfort her. Weeping because it seems that evil has once again triumphed over good. Weeping because there is no angel with her on this occasion, to whom she can look and ask, 'How can this be?' (Luke 1:34, NKJV). She is here, it seems, distressed and without answers, as her son cries out, 'My God, my God, why have you forsaken me?' (Matthew 27:46).

Jesus was healer, teacher, Messiah or blasphemer to others, but to Mary this was her son.

## Questions for reflection

1 What does Mary the mother of Jesus teach us about faithfulness to God and endurance in the life of faith?
2 How does she help us all to develop a more respectful and honouring vision of women and mothers in our churches and communities?

# Going through

I wish I had an answer for the deep pain we feel when we find ourselves bewildered at what occurs in our lives and in the world around us. During this final week of Jesus' life we are faced with a turmoil of monumental proportions. We cannot avoid it; the only way is through.

In the midst of my own great loss, a friend who had experienced the loss of her young child told me, 'Try not to judge God in the middle.' Her words were profound because, though we should not compare kinds of grief, I could not imagine how she had survived what she had. What she said resonated with me, because I was – and still am – living in the middle.

Many of us are 'going through' – a common phrase I grew up hearing in my church as I was growing up. It is often left open-ended in a sermon by the preacher so you can fill in the blank. 'How many of you know what it is like to go through?' the preacher will ask. Only you and God might know what it is you personally are journeying through: a time of particular fear and anxiety, grief and loss, depression and despair, loneliness and sorrow. To 'go through' is to journey through the desert place, where there is little sustenance and many hostile elements. To 'go through' is to be moving through a place nobody wants to stay in.

In the midst of disorientation in our lives and in the world, we might instinctively seek some comfort by trying to locate the truths we can use to make us feel more secure. This can include changing our ideas about who God is now that we have faced this huge pain or trauma. We decide in our grief that clearly God does not care for us after all, or that God is present but useless to help us. This might feel true, in light of the pain we are in. It might feel comforting, because now that we have come to a clear conclusion we can decide what direction we must move in. We believe now that it is all down to us: that if we do not make it happen, it will not happen. We believe now that we cannot depend on God for anything; we must rely on ourselves and on those who have a better track record than God in coming through for us. We hope that this might help us move forward with clarity, but often the changes we make can end up being over-corrections and simply another trauma response. 'Tarry awhile,' the Spirit whispers, 'you are still going through.'

In moments of great distress, our pain is often compounded by the feeling that we have been abandoned. It is a lie that, I believe, the devil (however we imagine this evil force) brings to our minds when we are faced with unprecedented pain. We rehearse Jesus as Emmanuel (God with us) during Advent and at Christmas, but not often during Lent or Easter. And yet it would seem that this is the time we need to remember this more than any other. Jesus in the manger is 'God with us', but so is Jesus on the cross. God is among us, incarnate and taking on flesh, experiencing betrayal, disappointment, loss and all that threatens to drown us in despair. In the words of Revd Pauli Murray, the activist, theologian and episcopal priest:

> God is never closer to us than when all our human efforts have failed, and we acknowledge our helplessness and defeat; when our lives are wrenched apart by devastating loss, and we are numb with grief; when our bodies are filled with pain and weakness, and we are compelled to face the inevitability of death. In our inability to solve the problems of evil and suffering, in our deep despair, we learn that our ultimate support and strength come from God who loves us, accepts us with all our weaknesses, and enters into our suffering with us. In the major crises of our lives, we abandon all illusions of self-sufficiency and find refuge in God's infinite mercy and grace.[1]

In other words, God is present with us in all the disappointments we face individually or collectively. God is close when we tell the truth about it. God is close when we are rendered speechless by the weight of pain. God does not abandon God's children.

And God is also with us, particularly those of us who experience pain and violence at the hands of others. There are, of course, kinds of pain that come to all of us by virtue of being human. But there is also a kind of weeping that is brought about by the actions and inactions of others, the kind of weeping that occurs for those who experience the injustice of the world. Jesus is God with this particular 'us', not just our collective 'us' as humanity.

The idea that Jesus is not only present with, but is also *one of*, the marginalised, oppressed ones of the world is very important to Black, womanist and liberation theologies. In these spaces, Jesus is recognised as being among those who are homeless, since he has no place to lay his head. He is understood to be someone who is hated because his life, message and values jar with what the elite of his day wanted to promote. Jesus is one who knows what it is to be born to people of low status, to be part of a minority group living under forms of oppression. And we can think of Jesus as one who knows exactly what it is like for the full weight of institutional power and corrupt systems to land on a person. As Jesus is arrested, he understands what it is like to be harassed by law enforcement and to be considered a threat when no violence is intended. As he is marched before the chief priests and Pilate, he experiences what so many do today as they are treated unfairly when they stand before judges in their own nation, because of their race. As he is mocked and paraded through the streets, he identifies with those who are innocent but incarcerated and made to pay the price for the decisions of others, in so-called 'joint enterprise'.[2] In his silence, he represents those who do not get to speak up for themselves when they face their accusers. Anthony Reddie describes this Jesus as one who is 'in true and full solidarity with all who are marginalised and oppressed and not only the ones who are deemed to be imbued with the requisite regulatory moral agency and respectability to be deserving of Jesus' care and concern'.[3]

In other words, this Jesus of Black theology is not one who is concerned with those who present themselves appropriately, but is aligned with those who are bruised and beaten down by the world. These are the people Howard Thurman describes as 'having their backs against the wall'.[4] In economic terms, they are the ones who live in poverty, whose lives are dictated by structures and systems beyond their control. Kelly Brown Douglas calls them 'the crucified class'.[5] These are the people who do not have the right connections to advocate for themselves, those who struggle for life and breath and for a good quality of life. They are the ones whose lives are considered expendable, or collateral damage because of race and class. They are the people who die and we do not notice; those who are threatened with death and there is no campaign to save them. They are denied justice, and only a few voices rise up to express concern. They are the ones for whom we shout, 'Crucify them.'

## The cross and justice

We can be tempted to rush through the discomfort of this kind of reflection by seeking meaning. If we can find meaning, we imagine we can find value and somehow this will make it all right. We do this with the cross of Jesus: we rush to emphasise the reason why it was good for Jesus to be tortured and murdered. We do not want to sit with the horror. But the reality is that there are many deaths that happen simply because people act out of violence and hatred. A woman is attacked by a man who singles her out in a secluded place because she is vulnerable, and ends her life. A group of racist men chase and kill someone else because of the colour of their skin. In rushing to make meaning out of Jesus' death before we take time to weep, we similarly rush to do the same with other such acts of violence. When we rush to talk about how great the cross of Jesus was *really*, we similarly rush to seeing the suffering of George Floyd as worthwhile. Surely – some may be tempted to imagine – it was a good death, since it has opened up conversations about racism. Did he, like Jesus, die so that we might live?

The problem, of course, is that too often the deaths of Black people have been considered worthy sacrifices. Never or rarely did the dead have any say in their deaths. Jesus states about his life, 'No one takes it from me, but I lay it down of my own accord' (John 10:18), but George Floyd did not lay down his life; it was undeniably taken from him.

It is clear that while Jesus weeps in the garden of Gethsemane, he is also somehow prepared for what he must face. He is aware that he could at any time call to the Father who would send 'legions of angels' (Matthew 26:53), and yet he restrains himself. He has chosen to endure this path for the vision that is ahead of him.

We can probably think of people who have endured in this way in our own families and contexts. Those who have worked hard to support a person as they tried to improve their life, to help turn a church around, or to launch a project or an organisation. Endurance is core to anything we hope to create and see grow. It can be difficult and can take much effort, even heartache, and yet it is good. This is the sacrifice we make for what we know is good and worth it.

Black history is full of such individuals who prove that some things are worth not only fighting for, but also dying for. I do not want to suggest here that Black people must opt for death and suffering or stay in such conditions for the sake of justice. It is a sign of the stubbornness of evil and unjust power that too often suffering and death are required before change happens. But Black life is not *made* for this; Black life, like all life, is made for the love of God, self and neighbour. When Black life is engaged in struggle in the name of that love, it can be considered good. But we should lament that such struggle is so often needed.

Sam Sharpe, the Jamaican Baptist deacon, is one such person who struggled in the name of love, justice and life. On the day Sam Sharpe was hung not from a cross but from gallows, I am sure that the people wept. Not the British Christians who enslaved him, but his true siblings in the faith, those he laboured alongside and for whom he laid his life down. It was Jamaica 1832 and Sam Sharpe was fighting for freedom from sin and death. This was not sin and death in a vague spiritual sense, but the very tangible sin and death that stalked him and his African siblings who were enslaved by British Christians in the Caribbean.

Sam Sharpe converted to Baptist Christianity in Jamaica. Unlike many of his peers, he was literate, which turned out to be essential for his ministry. He was a preacher, and was allowed to travel from place to place because the white slavers believed he was simply telling the enslaved Africans to be good slaves and wait for heaven. But he was preaching the message of Christ the liberator and God who freed the slaves in Exodus. Rejecting the 'Slave Bible', which had removed all potential of a liberation message, he read the full text. In his Bible, God turned rivers to blood and sent fire from heaven as signs that deliverance was on the way. Sam Sharpe and his peers were familiar, of course, with blood, shed not for the forgiveness of sins, but owing to the hatred of those who worked them to death or killed them in anger. They knew the fire of hatred in the eyes of their enslavers, who raped and whipped them at will. They prayed and they organised.

At the end of prayer meetings, Sam Sharpe would gather people together to share news about abolition movements elsewhere, and the message of freedom in the Scriptures. He organised a labour strike for Christmas of 1831, to protest against poor working conditions and demand pay. Sixty thousand slaves were committed to rebel in a non-violent protest. But they soon discovered the slavers' plan to break the strike, which would inevitably mean further violence in addition to what they usually suffered. Their response was to burn down the plantations where they laboured daily without pay, and to burn the buildings where their violent oppressors would meet to plan their fate. The rebellion was crushed in the most violent way, with only fourteen British dead and around six thousand Africans murdered, and many were condemned to death after the rebellion was over. This became a key moment in proving that slavery was no longer economically viable, which assisted the abolition efforts in England.

Sam Sharpe, and those who organised with him, did not allow themselves to be held back by disappointment. They took their lead from the God of the Bible whose words rang through time: 'Let my people go' (Exodus 9:1). Sam Sharpe would offer his life for the lives of his people. He, like Moses, would not step foot in the Promised Land, but his descendants would. For the joy set before *him*, he endured and would lay down his life for his friends. Delroy Reid-Salmon explains:

> The attitude of Sharpe and his fellow Freedom Fighters towards their execution illustrate their absolute commitment to the Christian Faith as evidence of being God's people. They gave their lives in confidence, dignity and courage in a manner similar to the prophetic description of the crucified Christ that the biblical testimony affirms: 'He was oppressed and afflicted, yet he did not open his mouth; he was like a lamb to the slaughter, and as a sheep before her shearers is silent.'[6]

This is an important part of Black spirituality and faith – the belief in a God of freedom. But also the conviction that freedom sometimes costs everything. This may well be why the story of Jesus' death does not seem surprising in the context of Black life, faith and spirituality. Black freedom has often been bought at a price. It might also be why, in Black theology, the cross cannot be interpreted as a symbol of God's wrath, or a celebration of the murder of an innocent person. This kind of God becomes no different from those who throughout history have murdered the innocent simply because they could. The justice of the cross within Black faith is in the solidarity God is seen to have with all those who know historically, if not personally, what it means to suffer at the hands of evil people and systems in ways that are undeserved.

The justice of the cross is also seen in the way Jesus' death vindicates those who suffer. Jesus is an innocent person dying on the cross – he has done no wrong, and yet he is murdered. But he is also God. In submitting to death on a cross, God reveals the ultimate foolishness of humanity. We not only do harm to each other, creating logics to support our desire to hate and exclude, but we would kill God when given the chance. In this, there is a kind of vindication for all who live under oppression in the world: the absurdity of racial oppression based on skin colour and ancestry, or sexual and gender discrimination based on genitalia; the nonsense of the exploitation of workers or the destruction of the earth, through which we put ourselves at risk. The folly of humankind is summed up and revealed in this moment. We as human beings are seen for what we are: not only often haters of those we can see, but also haters of God. And this is the sin that nails Jesus to the cross and leads to suffering and death for so many of our siblings in our world today. It is this kind of reflection that Black spirituality and faith leads us to: the connections between the Suffering Servant and the suffering neighbour.

## Questions for reflection

1 What conclusions might you have drawn about God, based on what you have suffered? What might need to be held lightly or reviewed?
2 Do your beliefs about the cross unintentionally prove violence to be positive? How might this be shaping your interpretation of suffering and violence?
3 What kinds of freedom do you hope to see, and what might it mean to learn from the example of Sam Sharpe as a Christian martyr?

# Epilogue: morning

Holy Saturday is a day of darkness: there is quiet and an absence of light, yet it is full of possibility. It does not seem this way on the surface, of course. It would appear to be a day in which death and evil have won. Nothing much is said about it in Scripture, apart from in Matthew's Gospel where we read that the chief priests and the Pharisees were nervous that the disciples would steal Jesus' body and say he was resurrected. They asked permission for the tomb to be sealed and guarded to prevent a 'deception' that is 'worse than the first' (Matthew 27:62–64). They wanted to ensure their violent acts would stand, and to prevent any opportunity for them to be undone even in the stories people would tell. They wanted death to have the final say over Jesus' life, and those of his followers, and all who might hear his story.

Jesus, the light of the world, is hidden away in the darkness, away from prying eyes and grasping hands. His followers are scattered and weeping, and even those who did not believe realise more clearly after his death who he was. But at some point, after the sealing of the tomb and the last trace of light is gone, darkness proves itself to be the prime space in which the Spirit of God is at work. The women have been tarrying outside; they want to remain close to Jesus even with the life gone out of his body. The guards have stayed awake in the dark, not waiting for God, but to ensure that those who love Jesus do not get too close. All is still on the outside, apart from these figures. But within the tomb, the same Spirit of God who hovered over the dark deep once again brings forth life, this time within Jesus' own body.

In this moment, we see that God who is Spirit is not prevented from acting in the world in which we touch and feel. Neither is God uninterested in the bodies in which we live. God does not raise Jesus as a spirit or soul, leaving his body lifeless and rotting. On the contrary, for Jesus to overcome the power of death, his body must also live. Blood has to pump in his veins, and his lungs must again inhale and exhale, if we are to have any hope. In this, creation will know that sin and death and the worst violence do not and will not have the final say in this world that God made and sustains with God's own hands.

And yet the marks of sin and death remain on Jesus' body even in the aftermath of his resurrection. The Spirit of God who raised Christ from the dead does not erase the signs of what he has suffered. Jesus does not get to forget, and neither do his disciples, that nails were hammered into his hands and feet, and his side was pierced. I wonder whether, in the days after the resurrection, Jesus suffered nightmares, or had flashbacks or suffered from post-traumatic stress disorder. In his humanity, we cannot imagine that this is impossible. Resurrection is not a breaking away from a history of pain for Jesus; it is, as Shelly Rambo the trauma theologian describes, 'life resurrecting amid the ongoingness of death'.[1]

And so we find in this an understanding of resurrection that is more honest and able to reach the reality of what we live as human beings, and especially as those who experience forms of pain and even oppression. This is not a moment for holy pretence in which the reality of what we have endured (and still endure) is ignored or forgotten through a kind of Holy Spirit-induced amnesia. It is a moment to look at wounds and scars, to remember them and to consider what they might teach us about the life in which God meets us and others.

I explain this elsewhere as core to womanist thought on the Spirit:

In retaining the scars of the tortured and murdered Jesus, the Spirit allows the scars of Jesus to speak of the violence Jesus suffered, even while his living body testifies to the ultimate power of God over death and violence itself. In the case of the body of Jesus, the Spirit does not choose erasure but recognition and redemption. In a similar way, the Spirit may also recognise and redeem all the sufferings of our embodied selves and those of our neighbours ... Where poverty, racism, sexism, ableism or heterosexism have caused wounds, the Spirit calls us to see and even to touch the scars.[2]

This is what it means for us to be people of the resurrection. We inhabit a world that is not yet what it will be, as people who continue to be formed into the likeness of Christ who embodied life and love in their fullness. The scars we bear are not cause for shame, nor must they define us in our entirety. They remind us of the work of God which continues to be needed in the world and in each of us, as we tarry ever more for the reign of God to be made known among us in justice and peace. They speak to us, in a whisper or even in silence, of the life we have and the life being brought forth in us through the Spirit, even while we tarry for all things to be made new. And as we tarry we cry, 'Come, Lord Jesus!'

# Notes

## Introduction

1 Genesis 2:10–14: 'A river watering the garden flowed from Eden; from there it was separated into four headwaters. The name of the first is the Pishon; it winds through the entire land of Havilah, where there is gold. (The gold of that land is good; aromatic resin and onyx are also there.) The name of the second river is the Gihon; it winds through the entire land of Cush. The name of the third river is the Tigris; it runs along the east side of Ashur. And the fourth river is the Euphrates.'

## 1 Darkness

1 Indigenous Values Initiative, 'Dum Diversas: Papal Bull Dum Diversas 18 June, 1452', Doctrine of Discovery Project: doctrineofdiscovery.org/dum-diversas (accessed 27 September 2023).

2 Chine McDonald, *God Is Not a White Man (And Other Revelations)*, (London: Hodder and Stoughton, 2021), pp. 137–8.

## Black and Christian

1 Zorodzai Dube, 'The Ethiopian Eunuch in Transit: A migrant theoretical perspective', *HTS Teologiese Studies* 69, no. 1 (2013): 4.

2 Brittany E. Wilson, '"Neither Male nor Female": The Ethiopian Eunuch in Acts 8.26–40', *New Testament Studies* 60, no. 3 (07, 2014): 407, 409.

3 Gayraud S. Wilmore, *Pragmatic Spirituality: The Christian faith through an Africentric lens* (New York and London: New York University Press, 2004), pp. 103–5.

4 Wilmore, *Pragmatic Spirituality*, p. 110.

5 Dube, 'The Ethiopian Eunuch in Transit', p. 5.

## Tarrying in the dark

1 David D. Daniels III, '"Live So Can Use Me Anytime, Lord, Anywhere":
Theological Education in the Church of God in Christ, 1970 to 1997',
*Asian Journal of Pentecostal Studies* 3, no. 2 (July 2000): 299.

2 St John of the Cross, 'The Dark Night of the Soul', Poetry Foundation:
www.poetryfoundation.org/poems/157984/the-dark-night-of-the-
soul (accessed 27 September 2023).

3 Daniels III, 'Live So Can Use Me Anytime, Lord, Anywhere', p. 299.

## 2 One

1 Robert Beckford, *Dread and Pentecostal: A political theology for the
Black Church in Britain* (Eugene, OR: Wipf and Stock, 2011), pp. 5–6.

## Dualism problems

1 Edith Hamilton and Huntington Cairns (eds), *Plato: The collected
dialogues* (Princeton, NJ: Princeton University Press, 1962), pp. 47–8.

2 Kelly Brown Douglas, *What's Faith Got to Do with It? Black bodies/
Christian souls* (Maryknoll, NY: Orbis, 2005), pp. 25, 29.

3 Harvey Kwiyani, 'Pneumatology, Mission and African Christianity
in the West', in Israel Oluwole Olofinjana et al. (eds), *African Voices:
Towards African British theologies* (Carlisle: Langham Creative
Projects, 2017), pp. 109–32, 126–7.

4 Chigor Chike, 'Proudly African, Proudly Christian: The Roots
of Christologies in the African Worldview', *Black Theology: An
International Journal* 6, no. 2 (2009): 223.

5 'Holy Communion Service: Prayers at the Preparation of the Table',
The Church of England: https://www.churchofengland.org/prayer-
and-worship/worship-texts-and-resources/common-worship/
holy-communion-service (accessed 10 October 2023).

## Embodying faith

1 Carol Tomlin, *Preach it: Understanding African Caribbean preaching*
(London: SCM Press, 2019), p. 108.

2 Eboni Marshall Turman, *Toward a Womanist Ethic of the*

*Incarnation: Black bodies, the Black Church, and the Council of Chalcedon* (New York: Palgrave Macmillan, 2013), p. 42.

3 Howard Thurman, *Jesus and the Disinherited* (Boston, MA: Beacon Press, 1974), p. 7.

4 Anthony Reddie, *Working Against the Grain: Re-imaging Black theology in the 21st century* (London: Taylor & Francis, 2014), pp. 75–92.

5 Rowan Williams, *Christ the Heart of Creation* (London: Bloomsbury, 2018), pp. 223–4.

6 M. Shawn Copeland, *Enfleshing Freedom: Body, race, and being* (Minneapolis, MN: Fortress Press, 2010), pp. 126–7.

## 3 Movement

1 Delores S. Williams, *Sisters in the Wilderness: The challenge of womanist God-talk* (Maryknoll, NY: Orbis, 1993), p. 3.

2 Joe Aldred, *Thinking Outside the Box on Race, Faith and Life* (Hertfordshire: Hansib, 2013), p. 199.

3 For a discussion on the Windrush generation's decision to stay or leave, see the BBC Radio 4 series 'Windrush: A family divided' by Robert and Jennifer Beckford: https://www.bbc.co.uk/programmes/p0fwnk74 (accessed 18 October 2023).

### Forced to move

1 Fernando F. Segovia, 'Biblical Criticism and Postcolonial Studies: Towards a Postcolonial Optic', in R. S. Sugirtharajah (ed.), *The Postcolonial Biblical Reader* (Oxford: Blackwell, 2006), pp. 37–8.

2 Anthony Reddie, *Theologising Brexit: A liberationist and postcolonial critique* (Oxford and New York: Routledge, 2019), pp. 120–32.

### Hostile environments

1 'Didn't My Lord Deliver Daniel?', public domain, cited in Antipas Harris, 'Black Folk Religion in Black Holiness Pentecostalism', *Journal of Pentecostal Theology* 28, no. 1 (2019): 115.

2 James H. Cone, *The Spirituals and the Blues: 50th anniversary edition* (Maryknoll, NY: Orbis, 2022), pp. 60–3.

## 4 Spirit

1 Steven Horne, *Gypsies and Jesus: A Traveller theology* (London: Darton, Longman & Todd, 2022), p. 28.
2 Willie James Jennings, *Acts* (Louisville, KY: Westminster John Knox Press, 2017), p. 28.

## The Spirit of justice

1 *The Apostolic Faith* (Los Angeles, CA, 1906), p. 2.
2 Steven Horne, *Gypsies and Jesus: A Traveller theology* (London: Darton, Longman & Todd, 2022), pp. 24, 26, 29.
3 Selina Stone, 'Pentecostal Power: Discipleship as political engagement', *Journal of the European Pentecostal Theological Association* 38, no. 1 (2018): 32.

## Abiding with the Spirit

1 Chichi Agorom, *The Enneagram for Black Liberation: Return to who you are beneath the armor you carry* (Minneapolis, MN: Broadleaf, 2022), p. 11.

## 5 Quiet

1 Howard Thurman, *The Inward Journey*, 2nd edn (Richmond: Friends United Press, 1971), p. 53.

## Embracing quiet

1 Roger Haight SJ, Alfred Pach III and Amanda Avila Kaminski, *Western Monastic Spirituality: Cassian, Caesarius of Arles, and Benedict* (New York: Fordham University Press, 2022), pp. 36–7.
2 Kevin Quashie, *The Sovereignty of Quiet: Beyond resistance in Black culture* (Ithaca, NY: Rutgers University Press, 2012), p. 6.
3 Toni Morrison, 'Lecture: A Humanist View', Portland State University, 1975, Oregon Public Speaker's Collection: pdxscholar.library.pdx.edu/orspeakers/90 (accessed 29 September 2023).

## Finding God and ourselves

1 Sarah Coakley, *Powers and Submissions: Spirituality, philosophy and gender* (Chichester: John Wiley & Sons, 2002), pp. 34–5.

2 Carlton Turner, *Overcoming Self-Negation: The Church and Junkanoo in contemporary Bahamian society* (Eugene, OR: Pickwick, 2020), p. 2.

## Contemplating God

1 Sharon Prentis (ed.), *Every Tribe: Stories of diverse saints serving a diverse world* (London: SPCK, 2019).

2 Calvert Prentis, 'Abba Moses', in Prentis, *Every Tribe*, p. 23.

3 Roger Haight SJ, Alfred Pach III and Amanda Avila Kaminski, *Western Monastic Spirituality: Cassian, Caesarius of Arles, and Benedict* (New York: Fordham University Press, 2022), pp. 30–1.

## Out of silence

1 Howard Thurman, *The Inward Journey*, 2nd edn (Richmond: Friends United Press, 1971), p. 53.

## 6 Healing

1 Candice Brathwaite, 'British Black Women Die in Childbirth at an Appalling Rate. I'm Tired of Fighting a Racist System in Vain', *The Guardian*, 20 April 2023: www.theguardian.com/commentisfree/2023/apr/20/appalling-statistics-black-maternal-death-healthcare (accessed 29 September 2023).

2 R. Croxford, 'Belly Mujinga's Death: Searching for the truth', BBC News, 13 October 2020: https://www.bbc.co.uk/news/uk-54435703 (accessed 18 October 2023).

3 See also Anthony Reddie, *Working Against the Grain: Re-imaging Black theology in the 21st century* (London: Taylor & Francis, 2014), pp. 202–3.

4 Ruth O. Oke, 'Healing of the Haemorrhaging Woman as a Model for Checkmating Stigma of People Living with HIV', *Verbum et Ecclesia* 38, no. 1 (2017): 3, 5.

5 'HIV and AIDS', World Health Organization, 13 July 2023: www.who.int/news-room/fact-sheets/detail/hiv-aids (accessed 29 September 2023).

## Healthy community

1 John Swinton, *Dementia: Living in the memories of God* (London: SCM Press, 2017), p. 12.
2 Amos Yong, *Theology and Down Syndrome: Reimagining disability in late modernity* (Waco, TX: Baylor University Press, 2007), pp. 245–6.

## Shared pain

1 Jarel Robinson-Brown, *Black, Gay, British, Christian, Queer* (London: SCM Press, 2021), p. 16.
2 Ekemini Uwan, Christina Edmondson and Michelle Higgins, *Truth's Table: Black women's musings on life, love, and liberation* (New York: Convergent, 2022), pp. 80–1.
3 Ben Lindsay, *We Need to Talk About Race: Understanding the Black experience in white majority churches* (London: SPCK, 2019), pp. 8–10.
4 Resmaa Menakem, *My Grandmother's Hands: Racialized trauma and the pathway to mending our hearts and bodies* (Las Vegas, NV: Central Recovery Press, 2017), pp. 4–16, 37–41.

## Healing together

1 'Child Q and the Law on Strip Search', House of Commons Library: commonslibrary.parliament.uk/child-q-and-the-law-on-strip-search (accessed 29 September 2023).
2 'Chris Kaba: Funeral held for man shot by Met Police officer', BBC News: www.bbc.co.uk/news/uk-politics-63767635 (accessed 29 September 2023).
3 Cole Arthur Riley, *This Here Flesh: Spirituality, liberation, and the stories that make us* (London: Hodder and Stoughton, 2022), p. 102.
4 Delroy Hall, *A Redemption Song: Illuminations on Black British pastoral theology and culture* (London: SCM Press, 2021), pp. 5–6.

## 7 Weeping

### Tarrying with Mary, mother of the Crucified

1 Diana L. Hayes, *Standing in the Shoes My Mother Made: A womanist theology* (Minneapolis, MN: Fortress Press, 2010), pp. 122–3.

## Going through

1 Pauli Murray, ed. Anthony Pinn, *To Speak a Defiant Word: Sermons and speeches on justice and transformation* (New Haven, CT: Yale University Press, 2023), p. 43.
2 The joint-enterprise law was created to enable the prosecution of those who encourage, assist or fail to act to prevent a person from committing a crime. In practice, racial prejudice is recognised as leading to disproportionate numbers of Black men and boys being charged and sentenced under this law, due to assumptions about them belonging to gangs, and being more likely to commit crime. See https://www.justforkidslaw.org/what-we-do/fighting-change/strategic-litigation/past-cases/joint-enterprise (accessed 17 October 2023) for more information.
3 Anthony Reddie, *Working Against the Grain: Re-imaging Black theology in the 21st century* (London: Taylor & Francis, 2014), p. 84.
4 Howard Thurman, *Jesus and the Disinherited* (Boston, MA: Beacon Press, 1974), p. 1.
5 Kelly Brown Douglas, *Stand Your Ground: Black bodies and the justice of God* (Maryknoll, NY: Orbis, 2010), p. 174.
6 Delroy Reid-Salmon, *Burning for Freedom: A theology of the Black Atlantic struggle for liberation* (Kingston, Jamaica: Ian Randle, 2012), p. 76.

## Epilogue: morning

1 Shelly Rambo, *Resurrecting Wounds: Living in the afterlife of trauma* (Waco, TX: Baylor University Press, 2017), p. 7.
2 Selina Stone, *The Spirit and the Body: Towards a womanist Pentecostal social justice ethic* (Leiden: Brill and Schöningh, 2023), p. 167.

# Song list

Music is an essential part of Black spirituality which cannot be captured in words. So here is a list of songs covering genres and different geographical contexts. They are not all songs that might be considered 'worship' or 'gospel', but each of them communicates something of Black people's connection to and dependence upon God, spiritual strength or the divine.

Sounds of Blackness – 'Optimistic'
Kirk Franklin – 'Blessing in the Storm'
Fred Hammond – 'Please Don't Pass Me By'
India Arie – 'Get It Together'
Lauryn Hill – 'Forgive Them Father'
Sinach – 'Way Maker'
Karen Clark Sheard – 'Balm in Gilead'
Cece Winans – 'Alabaster Box'
Wookie – 'Battle'
Hezekiah Walker – 'Every Praise'
Koffee – 'Toast'
Donnie McClurkin – 'We Fall Down'
Guvna B, DarkoVibes – 'Amplify'
Nina Simone – 'Feeling Good'
Kingdom Choir – 'Something Inside So Strong'
Nathaniel Bassey – 'Adonai'
William McDowell – 'I Give Myself Away'
Limoblaze, Lecrae, Happi – 'Jireh' (remix)
Bob Marley – 'Redemption Song'

# Bibliography

Agorom, Chichi. *The Enneagram for Black Liberation: Return to who you are beneath the armor you carry*. Minneapolis, MN: Broadleaf, 2022.

Aldred, Joe. *Thinking Outside the Box on Race, Faith and Life*. Hertfordshire: Hansib, 2013.

BBC News. 'Chris Kaba: Funeral held for man shot by Met Police officer', 22 November 2022: www.bbc.co.uk/news/uk-politics-63767635. Accessed 29 September 2023.

Beckford, Robert. *Dread and Pentecostal: A political theology for the Black Church in Britain*. Eugene, OR: Wipf and Stock, 2011.

Brathwaite, Candice. 'British Black Women Die in Childbirth at an Appalling Rate. I'm Tired of Fighting a Racist System in Vain'. *The Guardian*, 20 April 2023: www.theguardian.com/commentisfree/2023/apr/20/appalling-statistics-black-maternal-death-healthcare. Accessed 29 September 2023.

Chike, Chigor. 'Proudly African, Proudly Christian: The Roots of Christologies in the African Worldview'. *Black Theology* 6, no. 2 (May 2008): 221–40. doi:10.1558/blth2008v6i2.221.

Coakley, Sarah. *Powers and Submissions: Spirituality, philosophy and gender*. Chichester: John Wiley & Sons, 2002.

Cone, James H. *The Spirituals and the Blues: 50th anniversary edition*. Maryknoll, NY: Orbis, 2022.

Copeland, M. Shawn. *Enfleshing Freedom: Body, race, and being*. Minneapolis, MN: Fortress Press, 2010.

Daniels III, David D. '"Live So Can Use Me Anytime, Lord, Anywhere": Theological Education in the Church of God in Christ, 1970 to 1997'. *Asian Journal of Pentecostal Studies* 3, no. 2 (July 2000): 295–310.

Douglas, Kelly Brown. *What's Faith Got to Do with It? Black bodies/Christian souls*. Maryknoll, NY: Orbis, 2005.

Douglas, Kelly Brown. *Stand Your Ground: Black bodies and the justice of God*. Maryknoll, NY: Orbis, 2010.

# Bibliography

Dube, Zorodzai. 'The Ethiopian Eunuch in Transit: A migrant theoretical perspective'. *HTS Teologiese Studies* 69, no. 1 (2013): 1–9.

Haight, Roger SJ, Alfred Pach III and Amanda Avila Kaminski. *Western Monastic Spirituality: Cassian, Caesarius of Arles, and Benedict.* New York: Fordham University Press, 2022.

Hall, Delroy. *A Redemption Song: Illuminations on Black British pastoral theology and culture.* London: SCM Press, 2021.

Hamilton, Edith and Huntington Cairns. *The Collected Dialogues of Plato.* Princeton, NJ: Princeton University Press, 1962.

Harris, Antipas. 'Black Folk Religion in Black Holiness Pentecostalism'. *Journal of Pentecostal Theology* 28, no. 1 (2019): 103–122.

Hayes, Diana L. *Standing in the Shoes My Mother Made.* Minneapolis, MN: Fortress Press, 2010.

Horne, Steven. *Gypsies and Jesus: A Traveller theology.* London: Darton, Longman & Todd, 2022.

House of Commons Library. 'Child Q and the Law on Strip Search': commonslibrary.parliament.uk/child-q-and-the-law-on-strip-search. Accessed 29 September 2023.

Indigenous Values Initiative. 'Dum Diversas: Papal Bull Dum Diversas 18 June, 1452'. Doctrine of Discovery Project: doctrineofdiscovery.org/dum-diversas. Accessed 27 September 2023.

James Jennings, Willie. *Acts.* Louisville, KY: Westminster John Knox Press, 2017.

Kwiyani, Harvey. 'Pneumatology, Mission and African Christianity in the West', pp. 109–132 in Israel Oluwole Olofinjana et al. (eds), *African Voices: Towards African British theologies.* Carlisle: Langham Creative Projects, 2017.

Lindsay, Ben. *We Need to Talk About Race: Understanding the Black experience in white majority churches.* London: SPCK, 2019.

McDonald, Chine. *God Is Not a White Man (And Other Revelations).* London: Hodder and Stoughton, 2021.

Menakem, Resmaa. *My Grandmother's Hands: Racialized trauma and the pathway to mending our hearts and bodies.* Las Vegas, NV: Central Recovery Press, 2017.

Morrison, Toni. 'Lecture: A Humanist View'. Portland State University,

1975, Oregon Public Speaker's Collection: pdxscholar.library.pdx.edu/ orspeakers/90. Accessed 29 September 2023.

Murray, Pauli and Anthony Pinn. *To Speak a Defiant Word: Sermons and speeches on justice and transformation*. New Haven, CT: Yale University Press, 2023.

Oke, Ruth O. 'Healing of the Haemorrhaging Woman as a Model for Checkmating Stigma of People Living with HIV'. *Verbum et Ecclesia* 38, no. 1 (2017): 1–12.

Prentis, Sharon (ed.). *Every Tribe: Stories of diverse saints serving a diverse world*. London: SPCK, 2019.

Quashie, Kevin. *The Sovereignty of Quiet: Beyond resistance in Black culture*. Ithaca, NY: Rutgers University Press, 2012.

Rambo, Shelly. *Resurrecting Wounds: Living in the afterlife of trauma*. Waco, TX: Baylor University Press, 2017.

Reddie, Anthony. *Theologising Brexit: A liberationist and postcolonial critique*. Oxford and New York: Routledge, 2019.

Reddie, Anthony. *Working Against the Grain: Re-imaging Black theology in the 21st century*. London: Taylor & Francis, 2014.

Reid-Salmon, Delroy. *Burning for Freedom: A theology of the Black Atlantic struggle for liberation*. Kingston, Jamaica: Ian Randle, 2012.

Riley, Cole Arthur. *This Here Flesh: Spirituality, liberation, and the stories that make us*. London: Hodder and Stoughton, 2022.

Robinson-Brown, Jarel. *Black, Gay, British, Christian, Queer*. London: SCM Press, 2021.

Segovia, Fernando F. 'Biblical Criticism and Postcolonial Studies: Towards a Postcolonial Optic'. Pages 33–4 in R. S. Sugirtharajah (ed.) *The Postcolonial Biblical Reader*. Oxford: Blackwell, 2006.

St John of the Cross. 'The Dark Night of the Soul'. Poetry Foundation: www.poetryfoundation.org/poems/157984/the-dark-night-of-the-soul. Accessed 27 September 2023.

Stone, Selina. *The Spirit and the Body: Towards a womanist Pentecostal social justice ethic*. Leiden: Brill and Schöningh, 2023.

Stone, Selina. 'Pentecostal Power: Discipleship as political engagement'. *Journal of the European Pentecostal Theological Association* 38, no. 1, (2018): 24–38.

Swinton, John. *Dementia: Living in the memories of God*. London: SCM Press, 2017.

*The Apostolic Faith*. Los Angeles, CA, 1906.

Thurman, Howard. *The Inward Journey*. Richmond, IN: Friends United Press, 1971.

Thurman, Howard. *Jesus and the Disinherited*. Boston, MA: Beacon Press, 1974.

Tomlin, Carol. *Preach it: Understanding African Caribbean preaching*. London: SCM Press, 2019.

Turman, Eboni Marshall. *Toward a Womanist Ethic of the Incarnation: Black bodies, the Black Church, and the Council of Chalcedon*. New York: Palgrave Macmillan, 2013.

Turner, Carlton. *Overcoming Self-Negation: The Church and Junkanoo in contemporary Bahamian society*. Eugene, OR: Pickwick, 2020.

Uwan, Ekemini, Christina Edmondson and Michelle Higgins. *Truth's Table: Black women's musings on life, love, and liberation*. New York: Convergent, 2022.

Williams, Delores. *Sisters in the Wilderness: The challenge of womanist God-talk*. Maryknoll, NY: Orbis, 1993.

Williams, Rowan. *Christ the Heart of Creation*. London: Bloomsbury, 2018.

Wilmore, Gayraud S. *Pragmatic Spirituality: The Christian faith through an Africentric lens*. New York: New York University Press, 2004.

Wilson, Brittany E. '"Neither Male nor Female": The Ethiopian Eunuch in Acts 8.26–40'. *New Testament Studies* 60, no. 3 (07, 2014): 403–22.

World Health Organization. 'HIV and AIDS': www.who.int/news-room/fact-sheets/detail/hiv-aids. Accessed 29 September 2023.

Yong, Amos. *Theology and Down Syndrome: Reimagining disability in late modernity*. Waco, TX: Baylor University Press, 2007.

# The Big Church Read

Did you know that you can read

## Tarry Awhile

as a Big Church Read?

Join together with friends, your small group or your whole church, or do it on your own, as Selina Stone leads you through the book.

Visit **www.thebigchurchread.co.uk** or use the **QR code below to watch exclusive videos from Selina Stone** as he explores the ideas and themes of *Tarry Awhile*.

**The Big Church Read will also provide you with a reading plan and discussion questions** to help guide you through the book.

It's free to join in and a great way to read through *Tarry Awhile*!